WORKING ACTOR

My Brilliant Unsuccessful Career

Pat Beaven

"There are no rules of architecture for a castle in the clouds."

- G.K. Chesterton

Working Actor
Copyright © 2023 by Pat Beaven
Toronto, Canada
All rights reserved.
No portion of this book may be reproduced or used in any manner without the prior written permission of the copyright owner, except for the use of brief quotations in a book review. To request
permissions, contact meagan@rogers.com
Working Actor / Pat Beaven
ISBN ISBN 978-0-9953490-4-9 (paperback)
Cover Photo by Paula Kaston
Cover by Xee Designs

CONTENTS

ONE **BEGINNINGS**
(in theatre we call it the backstory)
1

TWO **OUT IN THE REAL WORLD**
11

THREE **DINNER THEATRE ... WHAT'S THAT?**
35

PHOTOBOOK
55

FOUR **GOING OFF IN DIFFERENT DIRECTIONS**
(geographically and otherwise)
61

FIVE **SUMMER CAMP FOR ACTORS**
81

SIX **WAS THIS IN MY PLAN?**
(was I supposed to have a plan?)
93

ACKNOWLEDGMENTS
121

One
BEGINNINGS
(in theatre we call it the backstory)

Four years old. Sitting on a little stool in the kitchen across from the ironing board where my mother was meticulously pressing the sleeves of my dad's shirt: "May I die a thousand deaths ere I obey one who wears a veil." With my line out as the Magistrate, I awaited one of my favourite responses from my mom, the one where Lysistrata affirms, "The war shall be women's business."

My mother was in rehearsal with an amateur theatre group, cast in the lead role in Aristophanes' anti-war classic. And as I was her only option for running lines when these productions happened, she had taught me to read years before I would encounter *Fun with Dick and Jane* and text such as, "Look, Sally, look. See Spot run!" I knew how to sound words out and did my best to follow along in the script, reading aloud each line that came before one of her speeches, which were underlined in red. Of course phrases like, "... seducing him to the cozening point" meant nothing to four-year-old me except that "cozening" was often a word I would stumble over. And I had favourite lines I loved hearing my mother say (Her exact intonation of "Oh, Calonicé, my heart is on fire!" is still with me to this day.) What I got from the rest of the lines, I'm not sure. I did know, though – presumably not through my own deduction, likely explained to me by my mom – was that the play spoke about the value and power of women. And I treasured this alone time with my mom, usually as she ironed or cleaned or cooked, while my two younger siblings napped. I sensed somehow that we were doing something special and *important.*

Just a little kid, I never got to attend one of my mom's shows (I doubt that my father ever saw any of them either, not being inclined to pass up prime tavern hours for an evening at the theatre). But one Saturday when I was about eight, I did get a chance to watch how pages and pages of text could be brought to life. Put on its feet. I got to go to a rehearsal with my mom! I say "*got* to," but the reality was that I *had* to accompany her that afternoon. I had been taken downtown to the orthopedic shoe shop that built the hated arch supports into the hated black oxfords I had to wear to correct my flat feet. My sisters were home with my dad, and my mother told me there would be no time to take me back to the apartment before her rehearsal. She said we'd have to take a bus from the shoe store to her rehearsal and that grown-ups would be working, and I had to be VERY QUIET. VERY quiet, did I understand? She brought along a colouring book with crayons and a little bag of marshmallows ("a quiet snack") to keep me occupied. Or out of their hair, more truthfully. And we made a stop so I could use the washroom at a department store before our bus trip – a little extra insurance that there would be no reason to hear a peep from me to interrupt the actors at work that afternoon.

Having been told that I'd have to maintain this silent and invisible presence for a few *hours* was not a happy thought as we reached our destination many bus stops away. The rehearsal was at someone's home, down in the basement. After apologizing for having to have a child in tow – and promising good behaviour on my behalf – my mom set me up on the narrow stairway leading down to the basement. The big space was empty except for a grouping of furniture near the centre - a small couch, a chair, and a coffee table. Someone was making measurements and laying down blue tape on the cement floor, marking off ... I wasn't sure what; the taped lines looked pretty random to me. More people arrived, almost tripping over the unexpected lump of child installed halfway down the stairs. Resigned to my fate for the rest of the afternoon, I dug into the marshmallows.

For the next three hours, I was mesmerized by the activity in the little pool of light in the middle of that basement. Peering through the railings, I watched men and women pacing back and forth, saying lines from memory or reading from the script, repeating sequences of action, listening to direction, doing it again. And again. Real people pretending to be other real people. Then taking a break: coffee, talking in hushed tones, laughter, relaxing now on the same sofa and chairs that had moments before provided the backdrop for the tense exchanges between the characters they played. And back to work again, with more repetition. I couldn't take my eyes off any of it. Colouring book and crayons never came out.

The play was Tennessee Williams' *Summer and Smoke*, the director, Marion André. This writer, director, and impresario had recently emigrated from Poland. Landing in Montreal, he quickly began work directing freelance for the McGill Players and writing for CBC Radio. (In time he would go on to become the founding artistic director of the city's Saidye Bronfman Centre before moving to Toronto to establish and reign over Theatre Plus.) But my first glimpse of him was at that basement rehearsal with his new theatre company, Studio Six. Where he had cast my mother as Alma Winemiller, the highly-strung Mississippi minister's daughter struggling with longings and an awakening curiosity about a different way of living. The adult situations and sexual content were far beyond my scope of understanding as I watched the actors that afternoon. What was indelibly clear to me, though, was the magic that was happening in that little pool of light. People looked happy there. Happy and frustrated and tired and at home and … happy. It was imprinted on my brain. I knew I *wanted to be in that little pool of light.*

It wasn't until high school that I got to experience a rehearsal from the inside. Or an audition or the whole organic process of making a show from scratch. Grade 8: my new friend, Lynda, pointed out a poster in the hallway announcing auditions for the school play. Except they weren't even *called* auditions; it read "TRY-OUTS FOR THIS YEAR'S DRAMA PRODUCTION! September 25th. In the auditorium." I don't remember the other details, just Lynda exclaiming, "We *have* to go!" Having had experience through classes at Montreal Children's Theatre, she knew all about auditions and was able to decipher from the poster what would be required. Breathless with excitement, she told me that all we'd have to do was choose a poem, memorize it, and present it up on stage the following Wednesday. Was that all?

I went home and started poring over our poetry textbook from English class – it never occurred to me to go to the library for a wider selection - and found something not too long that I felt I could learn by heart. I don't remember what the poem was or how much thought or practice I put into how to present it; memorizing it seemed enough of a challenge for me! Audition day arrived, and Lynda and I joined the hopefuls filling the first couple of rows in the auditorium. We added our names to a list passed around and were told we'd be called up one by one to recite our poems. I started to get nervous when I saw how confident and polished everyone's presentation looked. Lynda's name was called, and I watched her ascend the stairs and take centre stage. While I don't remember *my* poem, hers was called "A Lesson with the Fan." Lynda spoke beautifully, accompanying the words with strategized hand movements and what seemed like a staggering array of eye gestures: this was next level! I panicked, wishing desperately that I had prepared more. I wanted to run out of there. But no, now they were calling my name. My time on stage is a blur. Heat flashed through my head. I was sweating. I don't remember anything else except coming down the stairs and feeling like I might throw up. Decisions were made and results were announced a couple of days later. Lynda was cast in one of the major roles: no surprise. I was not (also no surprise), but was told I could understudy one of the other parts. I had no idea what that meant – not sure if I had ever heard the word before - but I was in. I was in the drama club!

Understudies were required to attend all rehearsals: listening, learning, catching the flow of the show, and writing down every note and stage direction for their character. How I loved those afternoons and early mornings before school! Sitting in the darkened auditorium, unpressured by having to "act" (I really didn't even know what that *meant* at the time), I got to witness how a show comes together. From the ground up. I was introduced to the terminology – blocking, upstage, downstage, pacing, subtext, motivation – all new to me, my brain was exploding. I saw what I thought looked good on stage, was amazed when suggestions from the director made it look better, stronger ... I was fascinated at the different cast members' reactions and interpretations of that input as they ran scenes over and over again.

And every once in a while, an understudy rehearsal was called. Terror. Absolute terror getting on stage, praying I could summon up the lines I had been working to memorize, hoping against hope the director wouldn't feel she had made a terrible mistake. My tactic was just to try to copy as closely as possible what the person I was understudying did; she was a big deal in the school's drama club and I felt I couldn't go wrong with that. So inflection, movement, pauses, even facial gestures – all absorbed and incorporated (let's face it, *copied*) - because that's all that I knew. It would be years before I understood anything about creating a character and making a role my own. But I guess it was fine for the time, with understudy rehearsals continuing every second Tuesday. And wonder of wonders, understudies got to play in the pre-opening matinee performance for an audience of grade seven students from surrounding schools. My first time acting on stage!

The following year I *did* get cast in the play. And the next year and the next after that. Working for hours in the auditorium, getting notes and actually feeling I was starting to know what I was doing on stage, being measured for costumes, watching the set take shape through the months of rehearsal, the ridiculously insane high of opening night ... it was all magic to me every time. Our director was patient, a good teacher, but firm and no-nonsense in what she expected from her actors. I worked to follow her instructions and answer her probing queries about my characters' wants and needs and the obstacles they faced. And a great chunk of my education came from hanging out in those auditorium seats when I *wasn't* on stage and didn't have to be there, soaking up everything she imparted to my fellow cast-mates. Total immersion – I think it's how I survived high school. I was addicted, obsessed. And maybe that's a necessary attribute for any wanna-be actor?

The first time I ever skipped school was for an audition I saw advertised in the paper when I was fifteen. The notice said casting was taking place for a new theatre company, and I felt very grown-up and excited to be venturing out into the real world in search of theatre activity. I slipped away from school during lunch hour and took the bus downtown. Then I wandered about trying to find where the audition was located on the huge, sprawling McGill campus. The little scrap of paper where I had scribbled down the address was no help at all. I had never been through those big iron gates or tried to navigate the maze of pathways, halls, and buildings. I just kept asking directions from students breezing by on their way to or from classes. Somehow I found my building just minutes before my scheduled audition time. How would it all go? I didn't know what to expect. (Maybe I shouldn't have *come*?)

I was greeted by someone who introduced himself as the director, chatting animatedly about Theatre XV, the company he was starting. Moments later, another fellow burst through the door, apologized for interrupting, but said he had something exciting for his colleague to see. And he had to see it *now*! He proceeded to unroll a large paper he had tucked under his arm and spread it out on a nearby table. Both men were looking over some drawings, pointing out this feature and that; they motioned me over to have a look. It seemed to be some kind of visual or architectural plan for their new mobile, caravan-type theatre. They were all caught up in explaining various elements on the drawing and sharing their vision. Their exhilaration was contagious; I got caught up too.

After about ten or twelve minutes of this, the director turned to me and thanked me warmly for coming out. We shook hands, and I floated back through the campus maze to my bus stop, high on the feeling of being in on the ground floor of such an exciting project. It wasn't until I was sitting on the bus on my way home that it hit me: I had never gotten to audition! Too much going on! Somehow, it didn't even matter. I felt I had done something BIG that day. (The director and co-founder of that company was a very young Peter Moss, newly graduated from the National Theatre School, who would go on to direct in England and at Canada's own Stratford Festival, take the reins as Artistic Director of Young People's Theatre for over ten years, and become an award-winning television producer and director. Fun fact: while I was at YPT several decades later, I got to share with Mr. Moss how crazy-exciting that day was for teenaged-me ... and also that I had since come to expect a little more from an audition!)

Once at university, I didn't have even a moment to get my theatre-fix. That is, not if I wanted to keep turning in papers and pass the courses I needed to pass. Not the strongest student, I had to funnel all my time and energy into rabid pursuit of the teaching credentials I was after. There was one play-acting episode halfway through my second year. I don't recall how it came about, but my French Lit professor – perhaps somehow aware of my love of all things theatrical? – ensnared me into acting out large portions of Molière's *Le Médecin Malgré Lui*, with him as a scene partner. In front of the lecture class. And he had a nontraditional, gender-bending vision, so I got to play the boastful, gluttonous, alcoholic Sganarelle, "the doctor in spite of himself." I memorized the French lines, we rehearsed ... I think I remember pretending to be slightly embarrassed about performing the instalments in front of my classmates, but secretly I was pleased. I let loose, went all out – this was so different from anything I had attempted on stage before! As a bonus, I learned lots about the genre of comedic satire. And it was my introduction to playing farce; I didn't know it then, but this was a form that would reassert itself to claim my attention and affection down the road.

Two
OUT IN THE REAL WORLD

I had been noticing newspaper ads for community theatre productions throughout the city for a while (although it was still called "little theatre" at that time in Montreal, before the pejorative "little" got chucked for the more grownup, presumably more respectable "community" label). Once I felt school was under control, I began looking at these ads more closely. I bought tickets to see a couple of shows. And I decided I might be able to do what the actors I watched were doing. Maybe? There was an audition notice in one of the programs for their next production, and that was all the encouragement I needed. I went, got cast, and spent the next few years bouncing from group to group, happy to have lots of stage time and be learning on the job constantly. So many personalities to encounter, so many varied experiences...

There were the suburban groups, well-established and organized, peopled mainly by middle-aged volunteer theatre types. Many seemed to be of British origin – people who always gave the impression that their birthright meant they had some kind of "lock" on all things theatrical – that could be intimidating. These groups had great subscription bases, with loyal audiences that kept coming back for standbys like *Barefoot in the Park*, *Our Town*, *The Importance of Being Ernest*, and *A Christmas Carol*. Once in a while something more edgy and controversial might be thrown into the season; *Five Finger Exercise*, my debut in community theatre, was one of these. Fortunately for me, shows often had a part for someone younger, and I got to flex my acting muscles and grow lots. But I was not an ideal community theatre member. Members were expected to take turns doing *all* the work involved in putting a production together: if you weren't cast in a show, would you be willing to help with building the set? costumes? props? taking tickets at the door? *I was only interested in being on stage!* A terrible (selfish) goal. "Every job is important! No show can go on without all the dedicated people behind the scenes." I knew that, and was very aware of my failing, but that didn't change the fact that truly all I wanted to do was act. Then I figured out that casting was impacted by this mandate-to-do-backstage-stuff: if a person had a role in two productions in a row, it was considered time to give someone else a chance to be on stage whether they were the best person for the part or not. That just pissed me off. So rather than taking my turn and intermittently being a bitter props person or a grumpy usher, I knew it was time to wave goodbye, with gratitude for the education and experience, and venture farther afield.

Next up was a production with a downtown theatre company, *Bousille and the Just*. A heavy, and at the same time, comedic play by master Québecois writer, actor, and director, Gratien Gélinas. Months of rehearsal, hard-working actors, and a preview performance never to be forgotten. The company had secured free rehearsal space Tuesday and Thursday evenings and Saturday afternoon at the Douglas Hospital. We had a large, bright space to play in, with a cafeteria down the hall that we could use for our coffee-and-snack breaks. Perfect, right? What we didn't know was that the deal was struck on condition that we would do a show as "payment" for use of the space – combo dress rehearsal/preview show – for the folks at the hospital. People on both sides of the arrangement neglected to take into consideration 1) what the play was about, and 2) who the audience would be that day.

Bousille and the Just tells the story of one family's attempt to save their youngest son from a guilty charge of murder, the result of a barroom brawl. Family members band together to convince the sole witness, innocent but intellectually challenged Bousille, to perjure himself in court. Led by family "enforcer" Henri, they pull out all stops, using psychological and physical cruelty to make him change his testimony. And the audience? Our rehearsal hall was at the Douglas Hospital, established in 1881 and known formerly as The Verdun Protestant Hospital for the Insane. In chairs set up for our preview performance were about two hundred institutionalized and outpatient members of the hospital community, there dealing with a variety of mental health issues. When the family on stage started bullying the innocent, slow-witted Bousille, a character the audience related to easily ... they reacted instantly. Protective, provoked, and angry, they leapt out of their seats and stormed the stage. The dozen or so caregivers couldn't hold them back. Cast and crew scattered, hearts pounding, literally running for their lives. Somehow we all managed to escape unharmed. Needless to say, subsequent performances seemed somewhat anti-climactic (and actually got to continue through to the end of the play!)

A few months later I had the opportunity to audition for my first Shakespeare production. It was the Scottish play. Our director, only six or seven years older than me, was considered somewhat of a renegade expert in Shakespeare and Elizabethan theatre. Cast as Lady MacBeth, I put myself in his hands to learn all that I could. I knew literally nothing about the language or speaking verse, and was daunted by stepping into such an iconic role.

The learning curve was huge. The director maintained that because actors know how big and important Shakespeare is, how the characters feel larger than life, that they tend to scale up the emotions accordingly; we would not be falling into that trap. Nor would we keep it all very literal and run away from the heavy feelings: in our production we would find the perfect balance. I learned that long phrases were often necessary to express these large ideas, large emotions, and large images … and that actors needed the breath control to sustain the lines of text. We were made aware of the need to play the opposites that gave life to the language and the constant puns, double meanings, and play on words in the script. The echoes and repetitions that were all part of the verbal texture. Specific direction with lots of interplay between MacBeth and Lady M – split lines and broken dialogue, where they are totally in tune with each other, one character's speech completing the thoughts of the other – was an education in itself…

M: I have done the deed. Didst thou not hear a noise?
Lady M: I heard the owl scream and the crickets cry. Did you not speak?
M: When?
Lady M: Now.
M: As I descended?
Lady M: Ay
M: Hark! Who lies i' the second chamber?
Lady M: Donalbain
M: (looking at hands) This is a sorry sight.
Lady M: A foolish thought, to say a sorry sight.

The company considered itself quite avant-guard – avant *avant* really – and liked to push the envelope. There was no gender-bending casting or catapulting the action and characters to the South Seas or modern-day New York, but various other tweaks did not go unnoticed. By either the public or critics in attendance. The three weird sisters with their incantations that we meet at the start on "the blasted heath" were played by a huge black man (as the First Witch), operating two hand puppets, Second Witch and Third Witch. Remarkably, it worked. And the simulated oral sex Lady M engaged in to override her husband's hesitation and push him to murder Duncan still had shock value in 1969. I think that scene was mentioned in every review our show got.

I had appeared in a couple of traditional British holiday pantos with the community theatre groups, but these were the only family shows I had been involved in. Shows that were loud, with lots of cheering, hissing, and booing as audience participation was encouraged from toddlers to teens, parents and grandparents, aunts, uncles, old and young alike. But I had never been in an actual *children*'s show. That was about to change.

The show was *Escape from Ordo*, an original script to be presented "in the round" for five- to nine-year-olds. A clever adventure storyline, colourful costumes, and flashy special effects all sounded good. Plus, I would have the fun of playing a twin and working with some amazing actors. What I didn't know when I was offered the gig was that this was a brand new script from the playwright and that he would be directing the show himself. I was new enough at the whole theatre thing that this didn't set off alarm bells and send me running.

Our director was a professional actor from New York who knew what he wanted and how to communicate that to his cast. At the end of our first rehearsal, everyone felt pleased with what we had accomplished. The second rehearsal as well, except the director decided there were several "small changes" that needed to be made to pages 1 and 4. We penciled in the new lines of dialogue and revised blocking notes to accommodate the set innovations he outlined. Next rehearsal, he presented everyone with new pages 5, 6, 11, and 17, and we all adjusted our paper-clipped scripts to include them. Two days later, the director showed up with a new actor who would be playing an added character written in "to help move the plot along." He assured us that this would a big improvement. Rewrites to pages 8, 12-15 and 22-25 came the following week. Never quite sure which version of the script we'd be working from – or for how long – cast members were wary about committing lines to memory. Which worked out for one of the actors whose part was suddenly revamped so that he delivered all his robot-lines in gibberish! With a week to go, a complete new script with various additions and "all the changes we've made together," was handed out. Oh, there was grumbling and cussing throughout the five weeks, but no one walked (although there had been talk), and that damnable show-must-go-on credo somehow carried us through. *Escape from Ordo* played to delighted audiences. And after, I never heard of the show or our playwright/director again.

I can't remember where I heard about the once-a-week acting class I decided to sign up for, but I felt some instruction was in order. I had been flying by the seat of my pants, soaking up all I could from job to job, and was beginning to feel like an imposter. Fairly clueless at the time, I had no idea that the instructor was a director/producer for the CBC – a fact that I'm now sure most of the other students knew. I can also see how that might have been their primary incentive for joining the class; having one's talents noticed by an influential television director could open doors. And at the time, CBC was basically the only game in town for TV actors. I loved the class and couldn't wait for Thursday night at seven o'clock. So many things I had been doing wrong! So many new ideas about inflection, pacing, sharing the stage picture, taking focus and holding attention. About *how this acting thing worked*. And at the end of the twelve-week course – surprise! – I was invited to an audition for a half-hour drama series. And then another and another. Small speaking parts, but it was my first time working in front of the camera. I was hired for several PSAs – public service announcements – for saving electricity, drinking milk for health, and voting etiquette. I got to watch myself on TV! I thought I had *arrived*.

Life was sweet. I was teaching and keeping super-busy getting my feet wet in all kinds of theatre ventures. I had moved in with my boyfriend of several years, and though the relationship had its ups and downs, for the most part, we were happy. Or at least that was the impression I was under.

One day I returned home from teaching to find my boyfriend packing his bags – his clothes, his sailing trophies, his precious box of chef's knives. He coolly announced that he thought we "needed a break," and that he had been offered a job in Toronto (Toronto?? When did all *that* happen?), and would be leaving that night. We weren't breaking up, he said … he just needed some space to figure things out. I was totally blindsided. Gut-punched. We would talk on the phone, he assured me, and maybe he could come visit for a weekend down the road a bit. V*isit*? VISIT?? Too stunned to say much, I watched him finish cramming shoes and sweaters into our (only) suitcase like this was a scene from some horrible movie. I remember watching from our little apartment balcony as his car pulled out of the driveway. I cried for three days.

It was the end of June. The school teaching year finished the next week. And then I faced the prospect of my much-anticipated summer vacation alone. Suddenly single (but *was I*?) and without any theatre activity on the horizon to distract me – no script to throw myself into, no lines to learn, no rehearsal schedule to give me purpose and connection. For the next week or so I walked a lot. Kind of aimlessly. I had long, serious conversations with friends over too many rum and cokes. Cried some more. Frittered away afternoons wondering what had gone wrong, what I had done wrong. Reading the newspaper spread out on a picnic table in the park one day, I spied something that shook me out of my sulky musings. "John Abbott College Announces New Professional Theatre Program," read the headline, and following was a whole article with a photograph of the director of one of my last shows. Who was heading up this new program! Obviously this was a sign!

My sweetie had flown the coop, looking for clarity, a clean slate, a fresh start? Okay, maybe that's what I needed too! Though the idea of going back to school startled me, I had been thinking for a while that some formal training might help me become a better actor. My mind was racing, my heart pounding: could this be the answer to *everything*?

I flew into action. I made inquiries the very next morning about how to apply. I filled out forms, and drafted then redrafted my letter of application. A week or so after submitting everything, I got a phone call advising me that my interview and audition date had been booked. I was really doing this! I found out that I had to prepare a monologue from a "professionally published play," in English, no more than four minutes long. Yikes … this was something I had never done before. There were lists of suggested monologues for males and females, and I just picked the first one on the females' list. I went to the library that night and took out *The Lark* by Jean Anouilh, in translation by Christopher Fry. I plunged myself into the tale of this simple girl, this hearer-of-voices, this unwitting martyr, Joan of Arc. I would never have been so brave or all-in if I had realized at the time how woefully unequipped I was to do justice to the monologue I selected; I just memorized and prepared to the best of my ability. And maybe it wasn't *terrible* (?) – or maybe the panel of auditors all agreed that here was someone in dire need of training – because two weeks later I got my acceptance letter in the mail.

The three-year Professional Theatre Program was divided into learners studying acting and those interested in design and production. My successful interview/audition meant I would have classes in interpretation, voice, movement, contact improvisation, and character and text analysis. Phew! Giddy with anticipation, I couldn't *wait* for the start of school in September. All the secrets I needed to ratchet up my acting game would soon be revealed. I had no idea what more I would discover ...

As most of my classmates were fresh out of high school, and five to seven years younger than me, they had come up through a system where Drama had been integrated into the curriculum – now a regular subject, like art and music had been for a while. "Theatre games" were nothing new to them. But the whole barrage of these acting games – relaxation, trust exercises, status communication, gibberish, murderer, and dozens more – perplexed me. Oh, I had fun with mirroring and tableau activities, but I was very awkward through most of these classes. And I wondered about the value of a lot of the work we were putting in. I remember an exercise where I had to cross the room as a steam-roller and I ended up portraying more of a cement-mixer (because I had never paid much attention, I guess, to the specifics of heavy-duty equipment). I got a unanimous thumbs-down from the class and tried to console myself by thinking I'd likely never need to take on a role playing either of these vehicles. But the thumbs-down made a chink in my self-confidence.

Months into the program, we learned about an activity called "The Walk" that had been planned. At the height of lunch-hour, as a class, we would stroll from our movement room, down the corridor, through the cafeteria, and back. We would walk at a leisurely pace, in a line, *naked*. The object was to get rid of any feelings of self-consciousness about our bodies, to help us feel comfortable being in front of an "audience," and to train/test our focus and commitment to a common goal. Told we could choose to opt out, I did just that. Partly because I thought it was rubbish; partly because being a teenager in the '60s – influenced by women's lib and the sexual revolution - had awakened enough confidence and freedom about my body that I didn't feel the need to prove anything to anyone. BIG MISTAKE. My choice not to participate was seen as a serious red flag ... what deep psychological hang-ups were lurking here needing to be unpacked so they wouldn't derail my actorly aspirations? I had to meet with program mentors to address my problem and my inhibitions. Appointments were made, we talked, I cried, and ended up feeling that my head had really been messed with. After a time, they uncovered someone else's perceived shortcoming to shine a light on, and mine was no longer news. Mercifully.

I tried to get on board with the notion that all our instructors seemed to be in agreement about: that there were definite unbending rules that had to be mastered. Without these secret basics that they were imminently qualified to impart, no real acting could happen. There were lots of positives. I learned about correct breathing and breath control, about pacing and pauses, about character objectives, and accepting the moment. The whole mystique of subtext and backstory became clear. Cast as the leader of the Greek chorus for our production of *The Trojan Women*, I developed ensemble skills. And a class that I never expected to enjoy became one of my favourites. Students in the Acting stream were required to take one production course, just as Design and Tech people had to take one basic acting class ... so each wouldn't be too stupid about the other side of the business. A whole new realm: I had an amazing time learning about bevel and miter squares, ball peen hammers, rabbet planes, and screw guns. We even did a project completing a scaled-down model of a stage flat with its rails and stiles, toggles, and stretched and stapled canvas!

I loved all the new learning certainly, but how much of my ... attachment ... to this class was related to the fact that I found the instructor very appealing? Curiously he looked nothing like the usual "type" I'd been attracted to: he had wildish almost shoulder-length hair, and a decidedly bohemian vibe. He was short, this highlighted by the tunic-type Indian shirts he favoured with hems reaching comically (endearingly?) way too low down over his jeans. As he was closer to my age than the rest of my classmates, we'd often end up sitting together at lunch in the cafeteria, chatting about theatre, education, philosophy. And dreams – those were fascinating discussions! The spark was unmistakable and took me by surprise. Maybe it shouldn't have. My boyfriend's leaving had fed insecurities about my attractiveness and left me vulnerable to the attention of intriguing men in my orbit I guess. I felt cut off from my boyfriend who seemed to be enjoying life in his new city so much that we had dwindled down to weekly phone calls and he had only returned for one visit since leaving.

My instructor and I kept whatever this was between us on the down-low (I think), until one night when there was a party at his place. End of term? Closing of a show? I can't recall what we were celebrating, but the delicious intimacy of being away from school, combined with wine in abundance and joints being rolled, made the exhaustion of suppressing emotion too much to bear. I almost celebrated too much. Moments after the last partygoer had toddled home, and I was alone with my instructor, I knew I was in danger. I hadn't given up on the relationship with my boyfriend, though goodness knows what was happening in far-off Toronto. I was instantly wary of crossing a line (oh man, I was on the very *brink*) that I couldn't step back from. After that night, going to class, sitting in the cafeteria, even passing each other in the corridor, became crazy-intolerable. A week later I dropped out of school, packed my bags, and headed for Toronto.

My plan was just to show up and try to put my relationship back on track. To see if everything could be salvaged and reset. On the train, I had hours alone with my thoughts. I went back and forth in my mind about all that had happened over the last ten months. And now I was a theatre school drop-out! I realized that my decision to go back to school, to apply to the theatre program, AND my decision to leave were both because of a man. Was that who I was ... someone who could just be buffeted about by the wind like that? By the whims of others? What was wrong with me?? I was disappointed in myself ... tears and recriminations as I watched the scenery zip by through the train window. And a sniffly resolve to be more self-determining in the future.

Fortunately my surprise tactics and heartfelt reconciliation proposal worked (I didn't feel I needed to muddy things up by going into detail about my recent close call that had highlighted how much I valued *our* relationship). Plans were made, new living arrangements settled, and Toronto was mine to discover!

The first thing I noticed was the *amount* of live theatre going on. Of course Montreal had lots happening, but French language companies produced most of the work. Brilliant theatres, large and established like Théâtre de Quat'Sous, Théâtre du Nouveau Monde, and Théâtre du Rideau Vert as well as smaller, populist and politically-mandated companies such as Théâtre Euh! and L'Eskabel. By comparison, English-language theatre lagged way behind. So opportunities to find stage work for English-only speakers was fairly limited. (Bilingual enough to order at a restaurant or speak in the street, I could not have imagined having the confidence or courage to attend an audition in French.) Now in my new city there seemed to be a theatre on every second corner. Large professional companies, smaller alternative theatres, and everything in between. I kept an eye out for audition postings; I was ready to wade in!

I knew I had to up my game. I found a photographer and made an appointment to have new headshots done, I revamped my resumé (that nobody would recognize anything on because all work had been with small, unknown, out-of-province theatre companies), I picked up two books of monologues and started searching for the *one* that would best represent what I could do to use at auditions. And I signed up for a scene study class so I could sharpen my skills and put myself in a place where I'd meet other actors who might be more connected, more in-the-know about what was going on.

And the chance for my first paying gig in Toronto came as a result of a friendship struck up in that class. Not with an actor, but with a musician and musical director there to gain a better understanding of how to work with actors. We enjoyed an instant rapport, laughed a lot through pairings in scene work and coffee breaks, and she invited me to dinner after a few weeks of Tuesday night classes together. It turned out her husband was an actor and knew a director looking to replace a performer who was leaving a show. Would I be interested if he could set up a meeting with his friend? Uhh ... YES, PLEASE!

Five days later I was on my way to Backdoor Theatre to watch a Saturday matinée and meet with the director afterwards. It was a children's show, *The Secret of the Magic Puzzle*, with a predictable plot line, typical baddies and goodies for kids to boo or cheer on, and a saccharine ending. But it satisfied the full audience of engaged and rambunctious 5- to 10-year-olds and their parents, and everyone left in high spirits. I waited alone in the lobby where the director said he'd meet me. So grateful to have been given this opportunity, I was anxious to make a good impression. My hands were sweaty, and my mouth felt dry. I tried not to pace. It had been almost fifteen minutes since the show ended. Everyone was gone. Maybe he had forgotten we were meeting? But no, moments later he was walking across the lobby to shake my (sweaty) hand and introduce himself. "What did you think of the play?" he asked. Wanting to sound discerning or savvy or *something*, I replied that it wasn't "great literature" but that the audience had clearly enjoyed it. "Let's go and read through a few pages," he said, handing me a copy of the script. I glanced down at the cover page: *The Secret of the Magic Puzzle* by Gino Marrocco. He had WRITTEN the play! Shoot. Now I *was* hyperventilating as I followed him into the theatre. (Note to self: Not a brilliant move. Going forward, try not to insult a director you're about to audition for.)

Backdoor Theatre was a free-standing stone building, formerly a church. It was small, seating maybe 150 people, with lots of charm and interesting nooks and hidden passageways. Space was so tight that there was a sign in the washroom used by the audience that warned: PLEASE DO NOT FLUSH TOILET WHILE SHOW IS IN PROGRESS! The flush resounded, somehow magnified by the acoustics in the space, and was very recognizable to those watching a performance. Inevitably, after reading that sign pre-show, there would be kids who hatched plans among themselves to "suddenly" need to use the washroom in the middle of the performance to create a little mischief. The audience laughed and there was nothing to do but laugh along with them!

I got the part and played the villain, a witch, with the expected cackles, creaky voice and black dress of rags. Arms, hands, and face were green, and I learned how to create some make-up magic with latex nose and chin prosthetics. I had never used false body parts like this, and was amazed at how flawlessly they moved with my face. And how effective they were in creating a scary persona. Sometimes too effective. Depending on the general age of our audience on any particular day, I might get a pre-show heads-up from the director: "Lots of *really* little kids out there ... can the witch be funnier today?" Or, "Bunch of ten-year-olds here – you can go crazy, scare the pants off 'em!"

It was a busy time: checking notice boards for audition announcements, making appointments and reading for anyone who was casting something I thought I might have a chance at. Acting is such a precarious calling: competition is fierce, with everyone always hustling for the next gig. Always that expectation, that pressure, to display talent and "rightness" for a particular role. I decided I had to rethink and reset my approach to auditioning. Actors have to get used to the rejection of not being successful at every audition. Only one actor can walk away with the role, and it often comes down to factors that are not even under our control – things like height, hair colour, personal preferences of those doing the casting. Advice is always that you have to develop a thick skin (a skin that I've never grown very comfortable in). Sure, it might build up resilience, but it can be a terrifying process that really takes its toll on your self-confidence. If you let it. Rehashing the way you said each line after an audition, second-guessing every choice, wondering what you could have done better, more dynamically, more ... irresistibly than someone else. Then waiting for the phone to ring. Wondering if you'll ever work again. Aside from determining to be smart about finding monologues that were age-appropriate and suited whatever I was auditioning for – comedy, drama, the classics – and preparing thoroughly, I felt it was important to choose pieces that I could relate to, material that *energized* me. But there was something bigger I knew I had to work on.

I had a clipping cut out of some newspaper or magazine article years before. I loved it when I first read it and had kept it folded in my wallet ever since: "Remember whoever is casting *wants* you to be great. They have to cast their show and are hoping they've found the performer they need." That made me feel hopeful and confident. I decided that going forward the spirit of this would be my new secret mantra. I would switch from looking at auditions as a means to an end, and see them as little opportunities to perform ... for a small, exclusive audience that was predisposed to see me as terrific! cast-able! *just what they were looking for*! It wasn't always easy to hold on to this perspective, but I tried, and I know it allowed me to be more relaxed, more open, and more able to show up ready to do my best at auditions.

What about the casting opportunities that weren't open auditions, where anyone was welcome to show up? Shows or roles you might feel you'd be perfect for, but you weren't given a chance at? Certain theatres and productions prioritized union performers or only saw actors who had been referred. I soon learned that there was some kind of underground tradition of crashing auditions – just showing up without being invited or having an appointment. I wondered if I could do that. Was I confident enough to pull it off? *Cheeky* enough to take a chance? I admired the boldness and swagger of friends who crashed auditions regularly, some signing in with a made-up agent's name or a story about a missed communication that must have resulted in their being left off the list. I did crash a number of auditions, but not with such bravado. I'd just show up, asking politely if they might agree to see someone not on the schedule, and then be prepared to wait around in case a cancellation happened ... or sometimes till the end of the casting day. I did get seen a few times. I think the idea made me a little nervous, though, and may have affected how I auditioned. I wasn't very good at it. I never got a role or a job that way.

Through it all, I was meeting lots of other actors doing the same thing. Only I discovered that often they had been sent to audition through their *agent.* Here was a whole new idea that had never been on my radar before. Who were these magical beings who found work opportunities for actors? Who were in-the-know about projects being cast? Whose job it was to promote their clients?? Did I need an agent? Could I *get* one? So many questions ... I knew nothing. And as it was before the internet and Google-knows-everything, looking things up in the phone directory was my main resource. And talking to people about what they thought were the good, the bad, and the ugly in the city's talent agencies.

I learned which agencies were the oldest and most prestigious, making deals for their established, high-level talent. There were the mid-level agencies, with client and talent rosters that weren't quite as top-tier; it was possible to send a submission to these agencies without an industry referral and there was a chance - just a chance - that they might agree to interview you. For those just trying to break into the game, there were various smaller agencies and solo talent agents who might take a chance and sign you if they thought you could be hire-able. Or if they liked your look ... or a friend recommended you ... or maybe if you brought homemade cookies to their office? I thought I'd start with these agents and see what happened.

I sent off my photo-and resumé package, along with what I hoped was an engaging cover letter, to the first six or seven names on my list and waited eagerly for interview invitations to pour in. None came. So I made the dreaded (but necessary, I heard) follow-up calls, and was told that "currently" they were only seeing actors with more credits or credentials or experience. No one had ever heard of any of the small, out-of-province theatres on my resumé, so that shouldn't have come as a shock, I guess. And of course I was a theatre school drop-out (!) so untrained as far as anyone was concerned. I fired off another slew of letters, and did get to interview with two agents, but nothing came of it. Whatever they needed or were looking for ... I didn't have. I had to get used to identifying myself as "unrepresented" when introducing myself at theatre auditions or slating in for TV or film gigs. I tried to make it sound like a choice: Look at me all defiant and indie! Fooling no one, but it made me feel better.

I originally thought that the big advantage of having an agent was that they could get you in to certain auditions – submit you for consideration - especially for film or television work; producers often saw only talent referred by agents. I learned their value went beyond that: they were also there to negotiate contracts, set out terms and conditions, and make sure you got *paid* for the work. I discovered how important this last function was after having to fight to be paid (not always successfully) for several small independent films I did. Some of these companies, struck to complete a single project – and impossible to track down when filming had wrapped - were notorious for taking advantage of actors eager to work. Lots of lessons ...

I continued trying to network (before we even had a word for it), to stay on top of who was casting what. Sporadic auditions – some successful! – resulted in random days on set for various film and TV work shooting in the city. After almost a year, I felt like I was starting to figure some things out. And then a complete fluke put me in touch with an agent. Someone I had become friendly with doing a couple of industrial films asked me for a favour: could I possibly stop by her agent's office to pick up a script for her? She was at her day job as a bartender and needed the pages to study for a shoot she had booked the next day. The office was close to my place, so I stopped by on my way home. I had heard of the Phoenix Agency - and it wasn't in the very-bottom tier of agencies I had submitted my stuff to - so I was stoked to have a reason to get a peek inside.

The office was downtown, on the second floor of a brownstone, nothing fancy. Reception desk and a couple of armchairs gathered around an imitation Persian rug in the outer area, two or three doors leading ... somewhere, just behind. No one seemed to be around to announce myself to, so I took a seat and waited. Soon one of the doors was flung open and a character who looked straight out of Central Casting ("Send us your best middle-aged-plus shady theatrical agent type") walked over to greet me. "You're here to pick up pages for Greta, right?" Without waiting for an answer, he motioned me into his office and told me to have a seat. The room was small, monopolized by an enormous desk. I sat down cautiously and busied myself looking at the framed headshots covering the walls. Didn't recognize any of his clients, but everyone's got to start somewhere, I reasoned. While the script was being hunted down among the clutter, the magazines, and stacks of paper and photos covering the desk – and what was that that just got knocked over, an almost-empty bottle of scotch? bourbon? – my host (I still hadn't been introduced) asked me how I knew Greta. He asked if I was an actor, and what I was "doing." I mentioned the children's show and made up something about a possible commercial I was waiting to hear about. "Who represents you?" Hoping to sound worldly, like some kind of maverick, I said that I was "currently unrepresented." Then, an introduction, and Wayne Meldrum asked why didn't I come and join his roster? Was *this* how it worked?? I didn't care. We chatted and I signed on the dotted line. I had an agent!

I anticipated life changing drastically; I was ready to be scurrying off to audition after audition for all kinds of amazing film work and theatre projects. To have the chance to be seen by important directors and casting people. And while I did get sent on a handful of "look-sees" for stuff I probably couldn't have gotten into on my own, most of the auditions I was going on were still things I continued to hunt down myself. I also learned that since theatre gigs were not the big money-makers, my agent – and agents in general – had more incentive to pursue the higher-paying film and TV contracts for their clients. And *their* ten percent. What I was really interested in was the chance to do theatre, to perform live, and keep growing my skills. But I knew I needed to play the game and threw myself into any opportunities my agent came up with.

I did bunches of industrial films for everything from charities to moving companies, drug store chains to Kids Help Phoneline, banks to vocational schools. And I had speaking roles on a number of locally produced commercials and TV shows. I changed my thinking about film and TV work not really being acting ... it was just a different kind of acting. A phrase from a comic essay by Woody Allen that I had read years ago made so much sense now as I figured out how to "modulate the broadness" of theatre acting to let the close-up lens do the work. I recognized things that I had to unlearn, new techniques to synthesize, adjustments that were necessary, and definite transferable, carry-over skills. I learned lots about being in front of the camera.

But I missed being on stage. By this time I had fallen in love with the idea of being able to fully inhabit another life – so *many* lives, so different from my own. I missed the luxury of prep and rehearsal time, learning to trust myself and my instincts to create compelling or interesting or funny characters to share with an audience. I missed telling a story in real-time, in one continuous block, rather than shooting lines and scenes out of sequence to be strung together in post-production. I missed the thrill and danger, knowing that everything on stage happened ONCE and couldn't be undone, rather than the take-after-take possibilities of film and editing. And I especially missed seeing, hearing, feeling the reactions of the audience: the laughter, the applause, and sometimes the gift of those moments of breath-holding silence ... of absorbing the energy of their response and sending it back out to them.

My agent was constantly admonishing me not to prioritize my theatre endeavours over kitty litter commercials and Canadian Tire training films. When I booked off for two months to do an out-of-town production of *The Importance of Being Ernest* (for which he'd probably make a grand total of $65), I worried our relationship might not survive. On my return to the city, I was booked to do a short film – a six-day shoot – and I thought maybe we'd be okay. When weeks went by, and I hadn't been paid. I spoke to Wayne; all I got was, "I don't know. No cheque yet." More weeks passed. I inquired again. Wasn't making sure I got paid one of the reasons I had an agent? His response this time was to scribble a name and number on the back of his business card and tell me this was who I could contact. What?? I left the office stunned. I did eventually call the number and the production office assured me that a cheque had been sent over a month ago. I didn't know what to think. I was confused. Then angry. But not angry enough – or confident enough, I guess – to advocate for myself and pursue it further. I never did get paid, and The Phoenix Agency and I parted ways. Unrepresented once again … ah, well.

THREE
DINNER THEATRE ... WHAT'S THAT?

Now unhampered by agent dictates, I was free to try to grab some stage work for myself. I regularly sleuthed the notice boards where auditions were posted, and one day read that Herongate Barn Dinner Theatre would be casting their new production in a week's time. *Dinner* theatre? In a BARN?? Both new concepts to me. Performing in a barn sounded like something out of an old Hollywood movie! I remembered as a young teenager watching *Summer Stock*, a 1950s musical on TV ... it starred Judy Garland and Gene Kelly and involved a down-on-their-luck theatre troupe getting permission to rehearse their show in a barn – and repaying the owners by doing farm chores (for which they were comically ill-suited, of course). It was romantic and magical and left an indelible impression on my 13-year-old self. Besides, wasn't Let's-find-a-barn-and-put-on-a-show something Mickey Rooney and friends were always doing in films? I needed to know more. And dinner theatre ... what was that all about?

That Saturday I made my way to Herongate Barn Dinner Theatre for the audition. It wasn't easy. It was miles out of the city, not even in a town or village, with directions that seemed all foreign and very rural, filled with terms like "Regional Rd.," "Concession Rd.," and "Lot # such-and-such." To a city-dweller like me, it sounded like gibberish. And being a non-driver, I had to locate a highway bus that might take me to my destination. At that time, none even came close, and I had to take a $20 taxi ride after the bus took me as far as I could go. Whoa, I guess only people with cars got to enjoy these shows!

The taxi turned off the main (dirt) road and down a small hill, where I got my first glimpse of the theatre. It *was* a barn! All weathered wood and very rustic in a lovely pastoral setting. I did kind of feel like I was in one of those old MGM movies, and half-expected Mickey Rooney to come dancing out to greet me as I ventured inside. Lots of actors, chatting amongst themselves, reading over pages of the script, and hearing about the rehearsal schedule and run-of-show contract commitment. One firmly stated requirement: "Because we're located where we are, obviously it would be too risky to hire anyone who doesn't have their own transportation. So it's our policy never to offer a role to an actor without a driver's license and access to a vehicle – that's why you'll see that question on the audition forms you're filling out." I tried to sneak a peek to see how this information landed on the roomful of hopefuls. Nothing. The producer continued flippantly, "But you all made it here today, so I guess that's not an issue!" I hastily checked off "Yes" to both DO YOU HAVE A DRIVER'S LICENSE? and DO YOU HAVE ACCESS TO A RELIABLE VEHICLE? Figuring I'd cross that bridge when I came to it, I followed the crowd upstairs for the on-stage auditions, determined to focus all energies on getting my next show.

A couple of days later, I got the call: successful audition (yay!), offer of a great role (yay!), and ... *we had come to that bridge* (uh oh!). How was I going to get around the whole "no driver's license, no vehicle, no hire" policy? And how was I going to get out to the theatre for rehearsals three times a week? I had some fast figuring out to do. First read-through, I bus-and-taxied as I had for the audition, careful to be let off down the road so no one would see me getting out of a cab. During our break, I mentioned that a friend had been coming up this way tonight and had dropped me off earlier. I casually asked if anyone happened to be going back downtown. I hoped against hope that my request didn't raise any suspicions. And I felt I could breathe again when our director offered me a lift. We chatted all the way to Toronto about what I had been doing, what he had been doing, about his ideas for the show. When he was letting me off at the subway and discovered we lived in the same neighbourhood, he suggested it didn't make sense for us *both* to be driving up, and why didn't he just pick me up here for the next scheduled rehearsal? Not knowing why I deserved such a miracle, I accepted with thanks, and said that naturally I'd chip in for gas costs.

Rehearsals were productive, we were making progress, people were fun, all was good. Until ... it ... wasn't. Rehearsal number seven: meeting my drive at the subway station, I slid into the front seat and sang out a cheery hello. The voice coming back at me was not cheery, "Could I ask you to drive tonight? I've had an awful migraine all day. I'd really appreciate just closing my eyes on the way up there." I almost cried. I felt so bad. I had to admit that not only could I not drive tonight, but that I didn't even know *how* to drive. (*Who doesn't know how to drive*??) All sniffly with my confession and apologies, I couldn't even make eye contact. Silence. Except for the sniffles of course. Then a low chuckle: "I can't believe you wanted a part that badly!" Not only did the director forgive me, he actually seemed to get a kick out of my bluff, and promised that it would stay between us. Maybe the surprise of those few minutes was enough of a distraction from his migraine woes, because we immediately tootled off to the theatre, no problem, laughing all the way.

The show, called *The Button*, was a largely forgettable comedy, but my first experience performing in dinner theatre was a revelation. From the homey atmosphere of the barn to the happy chatter of the diners queueing up for the hot buffet of roast beef, chicken, and mashed potatoes to the pre-show piano and comedy stylings of the owner as he warmed up the crowd ... this was something different. Our audiences were mostly country people from surrounding farms and nearby villages who came out with great loyalty to enjoy show after show. After we took our bow each night, one of the cast members would step forward to thank the playgoers and invite them to stick around and join us downstairs at the bar – people loved this. And then there were the bats that would be flying around way up in the rafters ... and would occasionally dive-bomb the stage. We'd hear a collective intake of breath from the audience as the bats whooshed overhead, we'd freeze momentarily as they entered the action on stage, then carry right on seconds later. What else could we do? We were in a barn!

Dinner theatre: a meal and a show under the same roof. A straightforward but deceptively simple concept, a phenomenon that worked on so many levels. Although it was all new to me, I found that it had been part of Toronto's entertainment scene for over thirty years, encompassing a broad spectrum of performance – from sketch cabaret like Second City, through specialty stuff like murder mystery evenings and Medieval Times, all the way to the production of full-length dramas and comedies. I was ready to dive in and explore the possibilities!

I learned about a few dinner theatre companies and began scanning the audition boards for casting notices. Most of the venues seemed to be out of town; my first audition was at an airport hotel, one of the homes of Gemini Dinner Theatre. My boyfriend had by this time become my husband, but making our arrangement legal had in no way mellowed his outlook on my theatre escapades. I somehow persuaded him to drive me out to the airport strip and locate the hotel.

Saturday afternoon, a big crowd of actors eager to read from the script in hopes of being cast in a British comedy, *See How They Run*. A lot of people seemed to know each other, some had obviously worked for the company before, lots of superficial actor-chat going on; I recognized no one. I was nervous but thought I did okay when it was my turn to read a few pages, paired with a couple of different actors. It was all very friendly and efficient. And I left feeling excited. We were told we'd hear back within the week.

I did not get cast. Not this time, nor the next *five* times I trekked out to audition for the company. They produced shows in several venues, always way out of the city for a non-driver like me. I remember one time taking the subway to the end of the line and then catching a highway bus that took me another fifty minutes to

Aurora; all the way there I was thinking to myself, "Am I crazy? How would I ever deal with having to come all this way on a regular basis?" That is, if I ever got cast! After each unsuccessful audition, I would get a phone call saying thank you for coming out to read for us – that they weren't able to cast me for this production, but they hoped I'd come out again to audition. I guess I preferred to think it was genuine and not just a thanks-but-no-thanks courtesy call, so I *did* keep venturing out. En route to my seventh audition, I recall wondering if maybe it was embarrassing for them to keep having to turn me down? Had I gone too far? Was I some kind of pathetic inside joke by now? So I made a bargain with myself that if I didn't get cast this time, I'd cease and desist and look for my next show elsewhere.

And wouldn't you know it? The post-audition phone call this time was to offer me a role in their next production, *Don't Misunderstand Me*. We rehearsed four times a week, and ran for two months – Wednesday to Saturday nights plus a Sunday matinée. It was the first of over thirty dinner theatre shows – often back to back – that stretched over the next decade. The work helped keep me sane and grounded as my marriage crumbled then righted itself and crumbled and righted itself again. It helped me pay the bills. It helped me grow my craft and my confidence. And it provided many adventures (and misadventures) working with a wide variety of theatre types.

I worked on stage with actors at every skill level. Some were at the beginning of their careers, happy for a dinner theatre contract where they could work, learn, and hone their skills; breaking into the mainstage companies could be difficult as they seemed to cling to the security of casting from a small, proven pool of talent. For seasoned performers, the dinner theatre gigs were something to fall back on, steady work to return to, between industry jobs. For the most part, I found the players were solid and took the work seriously, often rivaling performances seen on the best of the city's stages. Of course there were exceptions ... and cast-mates and colleagues with all kinds of quirks and "baggage" that made working together memorable – or challenging – or both!

There was the actor who fought such anxiety and stage fright that he would routinely throw up, then pass out for a couple of minutes just before going on stage. The first time this happened as we were waiting in the wings to make our entrance, I almost had a heart attack! At times during our scenes he would simply blank, stare at me, and say with casual honesty, "Well, that's all there is then." I quickly came to understand this meant that's all the dialogue his brain or his memory could access in that moment. The show was the murder mystery, *Laura*, and this line gap usually occurred when the two of us were alone on stage making sense of the clues to figure out whodunnit; exposition was crucial so the audience could stay with us. Which meant that I was left to fill in the blanks, saying things like, "Then I suppose you'd tell me such-and-such," or "So your explanation is that _____." I'd carry on telling the story, rephrasing his lines until the gap was over, and the scene could continue as scripted.

Another performer, well-known from years before to one show's producers, was hired in spite of her bipolar disorder – and the fact that she regularly went off her meds. None of the cast were aware of any of this, and initially didn't know what to make of certain backstage and on-stage behaviours. Her character had several long monologues, which she'd often play facing upstage, as if she wasn't even aware there was an audience out there. Or anyone else on the stage. Word perfect, but with an emotional pitch not appropriate to the scene, the pages of text would be delivered oratory-style, to the back wall of the set. At some point, one player or another would find a reason to take her by the arm and gently lead her back into the action. And the scene continued.

I played opposite someone who had no concept of "stage kissing" (or pretended he didn't). We were playing characters in an intimate, passionate relationship, and several kissing interactions were crucial to establishing that. Usually actors will discuss how this intimacy will be handled, so kisses look authentic without awkwardness or any personal boundaries being crossed. But at our first rehearsal, my scene partner just lunged at me, as if he was trying to *eat my face*. So we had the conversation, choreographed the various kisses, and worked out the technical details. Throughout rehearsals he kept pushing constantly, saying it didn't "work" for his character, that he had to "feel something." It's not like I didn't want our lips to touch, I was fine with open mouth, but no *tongue*, c'mon! The director and I both kept on it, pulling him back; the director told him maybe he just had to learn to be a better actor (!). It all got pretty personal and antagonistic. Opening night in front of an audience, when my colleague thought there was nothing anyone could do about his sloppy, invasive kissing, he went for it. I bit down on his tongue so hard that it drew blood. In the moment I felt justified - didn't feel bad about it - and never after that had to fend off his unprofessional kissy-mouth ways.

There was the actress who had a crush on our director, and was frustrated that he wasn't succumbing to her charms. After hearing rumours and seeing some close talk between the two of us on opening night, she suspected that I might be the reason for his indifference. Out for revenge, she (oops!) accidentally dumped a cup of boiling hot tea in my lap during our break at intermission. Shock and bad burns. Plus, my Act II costume was soaked and stained and we had to hustle to find something almost suitable that I could wear on stage moments later. To say the rest of the show – and the run – was tense was an understatement.

I did discover I had a weakness for directors. It surprised me because I had never been at all attracted to actors I worked with. Not romantically anyway. I found most of them loved the spotlight too much, talked about themselves constantly, and seemed neurotic and affected; that feeling that they always had to be "on" was a turn-off for me. But *directors* ... Okay, I had a weakness. I worked with some very charismatic men - they were in charge, they seemed insightful about life ... I don't know! British accents didn't hurt either (another weakness). Newly single – my marriage having crashed once again – I did become involved with a string of directors (not a *long* string) over the years. Not on the proverbial casting couch though; I pride myself on the fact that I never slept with a director until *after* I had been cast! True story.

Friends who were busy playing at regional theatres across Canada or in the city's mainstage venues definitely made me aware of dinner theatre's "image problem." Catching up over lunch with a friend one day, talk naturally turned to directions our respective careers had taken over the past four years since we had last found time to visit. "Are you in anything?" she asked, "Rob and I would love to come see you." I mentioned that I had opened a week earlier in a new dinner theatre show just outside Toronto. "Don't tell me you're still doing dinner theatre," she wailed, "It's nothing personal, but c'mon, dinner theatre? It's pretty lame." It certainly wasn't the first time I'd encountered this reaction. It was beginning to grate although I could see several factors that contributed to the image problem dinner theatre was stuck with …

Dinner theatre is tricky to classify. It's not mainstream or mainstage, it isn't given attention as part of the small or alternative theatre scene. Its mandate is not to present startling new examples of Canadian dramaturgy, or reconceive oeuvres from the classical repertoire. Critical coverage is minimal. The press seems to maintain a snobbish prejudice, and when they bother to attend at all, are quick to dismiss the work as crass or insipid. Dinner theatre is undeniably – proudly – commercial, relying on filling houses rather than collecting arts grants and government subsidies to keep the doors open. And as long as the myth of the struggling artist is alive and well in our culture, people will persist in seeing ventures that cannot support themselves as Art, and therefore the ventures that are worthy of attention.

But we kept selling tickets. Dinner theatre provided a very accessible theatrical experience for audiences. On several levels. The cost, for instance, wasn't prohibitive when you consider what the various components of a package would add up to individually – a meal, tickets to a show, and in the city at least, parking at two separate venues. The added convenience of not having to get up from your meal to dash across town for an 8 p.m. curtain (and will there be traffic? will parking be a problem?) made dinner theatre user-friendly as well. The atmosphere offered even avid non-theatre-goers a pleasant, entertaining night out; the plush and gold leaf of the Winter Garden might intimidate someone who'd never attended live theatre before, but let's face it – everyone's eaten at a restaurant. All they had to do after that was stay put and enjoy the show! It always amazed me talking to people after a show and hearing, "Henry and I have never seen a live show before. We laughed so much – we really enjoyed it!" This was something I heard over and over again. Perhaps there to celebrate a relative's anniversary or participate in their company's staff recognition night, dinner theatre was the first exposure to live theatre for many of our patrons. I always hoped their good experience might encourage them to venture out again, broadening and swelling the audience for theatre in general.

Shows continued, and between four different dinner theatres, I was working lots. Usually learning and rehearsing one show while the run of another played out. Shows would run for six or eight weeks, sometimes extended to several months, often having to have new people brought on board because some of the original players had contracts to move on to. Some shows were more enjoyable to work on, some more headache-inducing, some funnier for audiences, and some that touched the heart and sent people away with new insights or appreciation for a partner, a relationship, a stage of life. For me, all were adventures in their own way.

I did a show that no one's ever heard of called *Opal's Miliion Dollar Duck* (see, I told you!) about an eccentric woman who owns and operates a junk shop/jemporium. I didn't play Opal, but her best friend Rosie Montefalco, who reads the cards, tells fortunes, and loves to recall her days gone by as Miss Northern Italy. One of my favourite reviews ever – maybe "memorable" would be a better word – got quite poetic detailing the talents and charms of my colleague who played Opal, then added:

"She is always worth watching and I couldn't help but wish that she was telling more of the story. But it was not to be. _____, _____, and Pat Beaven were up there too. As Rosie, that last performer was okay. At least she didn't detract from the effort the way the others did, with their cartoon-like turns as shallow-but-cruel theatre types." (I was "okay" and "didn't detract" ... LOL, this critic was clearly not in love with what I did on stage. But another reviewer weighed in, saying, "Beaven plays the fast-talking, vivacious Rosie to the hilt. Her version of *Rock of Ages* that she sings when she sees Opal under a white sheet is almost worth the price of admission." So I guess it all balanced out!)

We did the show at a hotel where owners and dining staff were mostly Chinese. Perhaps the language challenge made it difficult for them to have a good grasp of what the play was about or why our set had to look so messy and chaotic, crammed with antiques, art canvasses, and every manner of garage sale treasure. Being organized and meticulous, as they were resetting tables and cleaning up at the end of the night, they would straighten up the stage. Items would be piled neatly, pushed into rows along the back wall, and left looking as tidy as possible. Making it necessary, of course, for our stage manager to come in early the next night to recreate the chaos of the junk shop. No matter how many times we tried to let them know the stage didn't have to concern them, it seemed they couldn't bear to leave it in such a mess!

At the start of rehearsals for one show, we learned that the play would be co-directed. Two directors, both experienced and having been at the helm for many of the theatre's productions, would share duties and alternate running rehearsals in order to accommodate their schedules. With this arrangement in place, we assumed that lots of planning, decision-making, co-ordination, and communication had happened. And would continue as we forged ahead. Tuesday and Thursday nights Marcia directed the action on stage, with her clear ideas about blocking, timing, and how characters related to one another. Rehearsals Saturday afternoon and all day Sunday were run by Jane, who also had carefully considered thoughts about how scenes should be played for maximum punch and effectiveness. In many cases, input the cast got from these two wonderful directors was *not aligned*. We would listen to notes, try suggestions, and play the action as directed ... and out of respect, I guess, for both directors, the cast became very adept at being able to rehearse Marcia's version (for Marcia) on Tuesday and Thursday and Jane's (for Jane) on the weekend. Only Marcia was able to be there for our dress rehearsal, so we knew what we'd be presenting. And only Jane's schedule allowed her to watch our preview show. As a cast, we felt pretty clever having been able to straddle the two versions, staying true to each director's vision. Until ... opening night. We had some fast and furious figuring out to do amongst ourselves, patching together what we thought worked best from our weeks of rehearsing. Both directors in attendance that evening must have seen a show they weren't quite expecting!

In Charles Laurence's *My Fat Friend*, I played Victoria Hope, a London bookshop owner. As the title suggests, Vicky is overweight. The story involves her going to great lengths to become the sexier, slimmed-down version of herself that she assumes will appeal to a handsome customer who has wandered into the bookshop and paid her some interest. He is off on a business trip and she has six months to transform herself, pulling out all stops with diet and exercise. To play the character, I needed some super-sized outfits to be worn over a "fat suit." My director created this garment, a kind of heavily-padded onesie that I had to step into and pull on before putting on my costume each night. It was remarkable, totally and believably changing the way I looked and moved. The only problem was that once the fat suit was in place and fastened on under my clothes, peeing was *not an option.* There are various theories about why the urge to pee is stronger when we're nervous or anxious (one I've heard is that our muscles tense up, and that includes the bladder!) Just before going on stage, I *always* feel like I need to pee – I know this is common for actors. Almost a pre-show ritual. Not possible in this show – nor was it possible through intermission, and not until after we had taken our final bows. I did doff the fat suit and baggy outerwear to reappear as the new sylph-like Vicky for the last scene, but the backstage costume change had to be so quick that there was no time to race to the washroom. We heard gasps of amazement from the audience every night as the transformed Vicky made her entrance on stage; they had never suspected a thing. That was satisfying ... and almost made up for the hard work I had to do distracting myself for so long from that insistent urge to pee!

One British farce, Not Now, Darling, by John Chapman and Ray Cooney, proved over time to be a sure-fire hit with audiences and consequently was frequently produced on the dinner theatre circuit. I happened to be on that scene at a number of different theatres and at various ages, and got to take on four of the six female roles over the years. I started out playing Janie McMichael, Gilbert Bodley's mistress, when playing "underwear roles" was in my repertoire. My next role was Maude Bodley, the wife, who may or may not be aware of her husband's philandering. Then came Miss Tipdale, secretary at Bodley, Bodley, and Crouch, who has seen her share of office escapades and works to keep everything straight. And finally, I played Mrs. Frencham, constantly popping in and out looking for her husband, the Commander. Don't know how I missed playing Sue Lawson (busy with other shows when I was at that ingenue stage?) and Miss Whittington (she only has a walk-on right at the start of the show and *has no lines*? Yep, that was the reason!) Doing the different roles with lots of different actors and companies, seeing the show from varied perspectives, gave me great affection for Not Now, Darling.

I've only ever quit one show, backed out after signing a contract, and that was a dinner theatre production. This was the second time around for the play. The theatre had enjoyed great success with it about six years before, and decided a remount would put bums in seats and be good for their bottom line (no pun intended, honest.) They felt fortunate in managing to bring back most of the actors from the original production. All except one, that is. Guess who was cast in that part? I hadn't worked at the theatre before, and was excited to join the company. I only knew one of the other actors, but all were very welcoming at the table-read and I was excited to start rehearsals. Same director, and it seemed like blocking came back easily to the group; running scenes, this actor or that would contribute some direction or bit of business recalled from their long-ago show. This should've been a red flag.

When it came time for my first entrance, I heard, "Oh, remember how Elly used to walk in with that huge sigh and just stand there staring out front for like, *seconds*?" Another voice: "The audience just ate that up!" (Hmm, okay … nice that they appreciated their colleague's stage skills …but let's move along.) A page or two later: "Wasn't this where Elly would not notice the ottoman and just kind of stumble over it without missing a beat?" And there was more …

"Remember how she'd keep arranging all the cushions behind her on the couch to try to get comfortable?"

"Didn't Elly pause and look at the open door before saying that line?"

(director asks me to try the line that way)

"Elly would pace back and forth there. That always got a laugh!"

(nodding, the director directs me to pace)

And I could go on. I left rehearsal feeling *down* – down about the role, about my ability to live up to all the "Elly-ness" people were missing, about how this would all resolve itself. I tried to justify everything, normalizing the reminiscing and even respecting the actors' admiration for a former cast-mate.

But when the second rehearsal went the same way, with actors continuing to throw around "helpful" comments and suggestions, I realized that I hadn't been hired to play the part, but to play Elly-playing-the-part. I contemplated a dramatic exit, with me countering one of their trotted-out remembrances with an emotional, "What's the matter, was ELLY *not available* to do the role??" Then I'd leave the stage and swan out of the theatre without so much as a backward glance. Not given much to histrionics, though, I just had a quiet word with the producer, and was once again hustling for my next show.

Comedies are perennially popular on the dinner theatre circuit, providing an entertaining evening and easy laughter for audiences. Farce, a particular type of comedy and a genre unto itself, is a mainstay. I've heard farce described as ordinary people caught in extraordinary circumstances, and that may be as good an explanation as any. All kinds of miscommunication and mistaken identity, reversals of logic, absurd plots, and exaggerated reactions happen – often at a breakneck pace – as trousers are dropped, doors are slammed, and the vicar discovers someone's scantily-clad mistress behind the drinks cabinet. (Actors often joke that they're all the same play – just with different titles. Maybe that's why it's sometimes challenging to remember the names of some shows I've done, to distinguish which was which.)

Farce has been around since Greco-Latin times when Terence and Plautus were writing and through the commedia del'arte influenced European writers such as Molière, Feydeau, and others. The enjoyment of farce doesn't require great sensitivity or intelligence in an audience, and doesn't presume knowledge of history, literature, politics or religion. Maybe that accounts for the low regard in which it can be held? Among actors, playing farce is often dismissed as an easy job, not requiring any particular effort or expertise. Kind of at the bottom of the acting skills hierarchy. But that's not where it belongs.

I feel so lucky to have shared the stage with certain actors and directors who understood and appreciated the rigorous demands and discipline of playing farce. Watching them, working alongside them, observing at close range as they pulled tricks and techniques out of their back pockets taught me more than I ever could have learned from any book or theatre course. The crucial elements of farce acting: creating an easily-recognizable "type" without presenting a cardboard character, the world of physical comedy, timing and tempo, and the magic of "playing" with the audience ... on-the-job training par excellence! It was like a master class.

I absorbed all that I could and tried to incorporate this new learning, to layer it into what I did on stage. One actor was an expert at the extended "look," the take, and the double take; I practiced what I saw and found new ways to communicate with an audience. Another performer I worked with was fearless in his use of physical humour: his flexibility and inventiveness in leaping over the back of a couch or banging into an open door gave me the courage to try dropping my own bits of business into scenes I played. Chasing people, bumping into furniture, throwing and breaking things, tripping, falling down, walking funny ... just a few of the rudiments of physical comedy I had the opportunity to study up close as I rehearsed with various talented actors. A keen awareness of how props could best be manipulated for comic effect was another gem. And as the old joke goes, "What are the three most important elements of comedy?" The answer, of course, is: "Timing, timing, and timing." In some forms of drama, a mediocre actor who delivers lines with no sense of timing and slows the pace by not picking up cues can often get by. The performance might be carried by the significance of the storyline, or the interest generated by the relationship between the characters on stage. In farce, there's no such luxury. The actor tests herself constantly: every fourth or fifth line is a laugh line and must be delivered with impeccable timing to succeed. Often in farce, as the action escalates and disaster follows disaster, laughs tend to "pile up." To avoid slowing the pace and losing momentum, the actor must be in control, deciding which laughs to play down and which will be given full treatment. These are solid *skills*, and I'm so grateful for all my informal teachers – generous dinner theatre actors I got to share stages with over the years.

PHOTOBOOK

first headshot, 19 years old

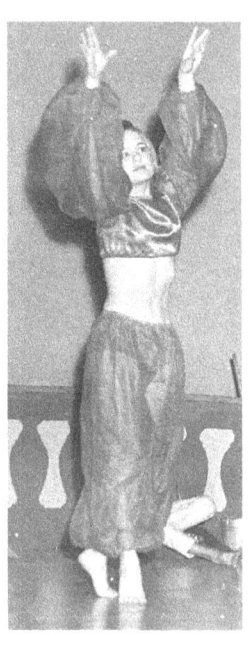
British pantomime: Sinbad the Sailor

lots of comedies!

dinner theatre production, My Fat Friend

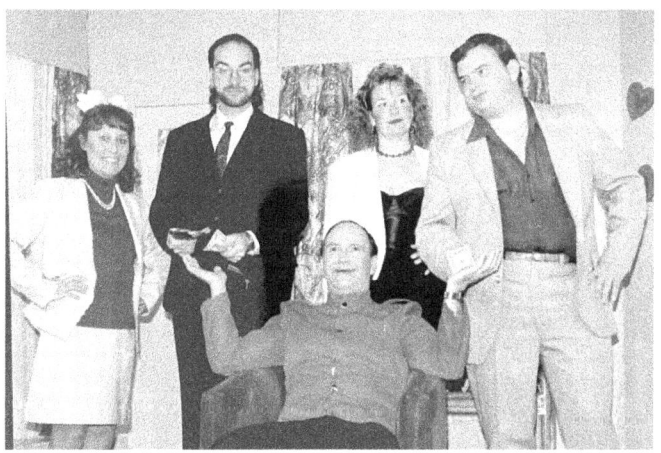

on stage... in good company!

*getting notes backstage:
Steel Magnolias*

february 10th
we opened! "gingerbread lady"
up & running. absolutely exhausted
from late-night rehearsals all week
and filled with trepidation about
① so many lines, cues, bits of
business to get right, ② audience
buying (& liking) the whole evry
character... of my portrayal of
evy, i guess, and ③ how the audience would respond to the nature
of the show itself (heavier and
darker than usual dinner theatre
fare) ALL WENT WELL!
and good to hear response
to humorous lines in the very
darkest sections...

so now we play!
onward & upward!

transforming, "becoming"
Rosie Montefalco for
Opal's Million Dollar Duck

Gemini Dinner Theatre:
Murder at the Howard Johnsons

TV series – wardrobe call

The Importance of Being Earnest

faces of a director!

Four
GOING OFF IN DIFFERENT DIRECTIONS
(geographically and otherwise)

I was teaching part-time, keeping busy with stage work, trying to balance work, play, friends, and family life. As we do. My marriage, always on the turbulent side, seemed fairly stable as we settled into our role as new parents; our baby daughter's arrival may have given us both reasons to feel more anchored in the relationship. My husband was still not a fan of my love affair with the theatre ... and while he expected support for his interests and career choices, he considered mine as something to be tolerated at best. I knew that from the start and had come to realize that it likely wouldn't change. What I didn't see coming was news that my husband had been offered – and accepted - a job contract across the country. And that we would be packing up our family and moving to Halifax in a month's time! (The decision to uproot one's life to follow a guy kind of went against all the notions of being an independent woman I had grown up with, but I was young and just doing my best to make everything work.) I tried to look on it as a family adventure, but didn't know how much of an adventure it would turn out to be.

We arrived on the East Coast in mid-winter to blustery, blizzardy weather we had never experienced before. And the house we rented was miles outside the downtown core (although coming from a large metropolis like Toronto, downtown Halifax didn't seem very "downtown" to me); it was close to where my husband would be working as head of food services for the university. The next few days were spent finding places for the basic pieces of furniture we had brought with us, unpacking boxes, and helping the cat and our one-year-old settle into their new home. That weekend my husband picked up the local newspaper so we'd get an idea of what was going on. Page 8: a little box, 2 inches square – so small I almost missed it: "OPEN AUDITION - New original work based on the life of Helen Creighton." It went on to give details of time and place, and I think some number to call for more information. It was a blur - all I saw was that there was an audition (maybe Halifax wouldn't be so bad after all?) ... and that it was the *next* day! Of course it was madness to think of zipping off to something so unexpected and *frivolous* in the middle of our big move, but I guess even my husband saw that it might ease the sting for me of feeling cut off from my theatre work in Toronto. Uncharacteristically, he said he could be on baby-duty, and he actually drove me to the 3 p.m. audition the following day.

Just a handful of people in the theatre when I arrived – a dozen or so actors ready to audition, plus director, producer, playwright, and a few others who we weren't introduced to ... maybe readers we'd be paired with? Everyone was busy looking over the photocopied script pages handed out. I learned the show was about the life of Helen Creighton – *Dr.* Helen Creighton. I remembered reading that name in the audition notice – it meant nothing to me at the time and meant nothing to me now ... except that now I was about to try to *be* this person, reading from the script. (I had never heard the name before, but soon discovered that all Maritimers studied Creighton's work and legend from the time they were schoolchildren. This prominent Canadian folklorist documented and preserved sea shanties, stories, customs, and superstitions as she traveled around Nova Scotia in the early 1900s; she authored books like *Bluenose Ghosts* and *Folklore of Lunenburg County*.) But I didn't know any of that when I went up on stage to read – just did my best: cold readings have always been my favourite way to audition anyway.

I was first! Up on stage, I read two scenes with various actors ... listened to a little direction after the second scene: could I try this line with a different affect, another energy? Well, of course, why not? Then: "Great. Thanks. Come on down to the piano and sing something for us." Whoa, wait a minute, what?

"Oh, I'm sorry ... I don't sing."

"This is a musical. I'm sure you can sing. Just sing anything for us."

"No really, I can't sing. I would never have come if I knew it was a musical."

"Just sing ... *Happy Birthday*. Sing anything." (pianist begins playing through a few bars, looking at me expectantly)

"Okay, you asked for it." (singing ... the way I sing ...)

"Ah, you really *don't* sing. Thanks so much for coming out to read anyway."

"Sorry to waste your time. In the future, maybe it would be helpful to include that you're casting a musical in the audition notice. Just a thought? Ok, thanks, 'bye." (gathering up coat, hat, scarf, and mitts and slinking away into the cold Halifax afternoon.)

A week later, the phone rang. Could I come to the theatre to meet? Thinking they must have dialed the wrong number, I reminded the caller, "Uhh, I'm the one who doesn't sing, remember?" They confirmed that they had the right number and I agreed to go back to see them the next day. I was curious. And what I heard when I met in person with the director, producer, and playwright took me by surprise. They said their entire show had been cast for months but they hadn't been able to find the right person to play the young Helen Creighton (another actor would play her in middle age and beyond). And they felt I *was that person.* In fact they felt so strongly about it that they were going to rewrite all of Helen's songs so they could be delegated to other characters. If I was still interested? Shock, for sure. But hell, yeah – when else would I ever be offered the chance to star in a musical without having to sing a single note?!

Rehearsals started the next week – a big cast (and I think only a few actors whose noses were out of joint because the role had been given to someone from "outside" who didn't even know who Helen Creighton *was* until the week before). I got to see how a musical was put together from the ground up, how dance and fencing sequences were rehearsed into the action, how the musical numbers were layered in. The Maritime heritage music was brought to life by guitar, organ, soloists, plus two large choirs of about two dozen singers each. And excitement ran high when news came that well-known folksinger Clary Croft would be joining the cast as The Fisherman, whose reminiscing starts the show with his rendition of the traditional tune *Drimindown*. I even got to join everyone for the big musical finale, where my voice could be drowned out by the talented professionals on stage singing *Farewell to Nova Scotia*.

The real Helen Creighton, who was 82 at the time, was invited to watch our dress rehearsal and be a guest at the first performance. I was nervous, hoping my portrayal would seem authentic, something she approved of. Sitting in the theatre seats after dress rehearsal, we had a chance to chat and I asked her what it felt like to see herself played by someone else on stage. She said she was thrilled, pointing out that people didn't usually have that honour until after they were dead. Opening night was a grand affair: a kilted piper led in Dr. Creighton, the Lieutenant-Governor, and assorted dignitaries, press were in attendance, and CBC came to film various sequences for *Newsday*. Musical theatre + me ... who knew?!

Next move was also the result of a decision made unilaterally (I know, I know – dysfunctional coupledom, what can I say?) My husband applied to go back to school to study economics. At Brock University in St. Catharines, Ontario. So we picked up, packed up, and settled into this small but growing almost-city. At that time, it was pretty much a university town, and anything in the arts or theatre happened through the university. After Toronto, it seemed like a cultural *desert*. Oh, I was told the Ice Capades did come through every January ... so there was that. Being suddenly student-poor, my husband and I both needed to find jobs immediately, jobs that would fit in with his school schedule and allow us to alternate caring for our toddler. We were hired within a day or two – he would be a bouncer and I would work various shifts as a server at a downtown bar. So we had an income, life was hectic but manageable, and months flew by (almost time to book tickets for those Ice Capades.). One day I woke up and realized I'd go crazy serving draft beer and trays of shooters forever. There must be *something* else I could do? Listening to the radio while building block towers with my daughter that afternoon gave me an idea. Radio! There were a couple of local stations ... why couldn't I find work there? I wouldn't be on stage, but it was performing of sorts ... I'd be using my voice ... it never occurred to me to worry that I'd never done it before and knew nothing about being on air.

I grabbed the phone directory and made calls to the three local radio stations. Announcing that I was calling to inquire about the possibility of a job, I was asked what my typing speed was. "No, no ... I'm looking for something on air." Then: "Do you have radio experience?" When I admitted I did not, maybe I only imagined the receptionist rolling her eyes in derision as she told me they "weren't really hiring at the moment." That was at the first two stations I called. The third receptionist chatted with me for a couple of minutes and then asked, "Would you be able to come in and meet with the station manager at ten tomorrow morning?"

Bright and early the next day I walked through the doors of CHSC, Radio 1220. I was ushered upstairs to the station manager's office. Mr. Redmond explained that they were in the process of developing a late-night show that would air between 11:30 – 1:30, a mix of prose and poetry readings interspersed with easy-listening music. They were looking a female voice to be featured; he said they had narrowed it down to seven performers and that the board would meet that night to review the tapes and make a decision. Would I be interested in auditioning? It sounded too good to be true ... yes, of course I would! Next question, "Do you have any poetry with you?" (asked as if this was a perfectly normal query and that most people might just be walking around with a volume of poetry tucked in their bag or back pocket). "No? No problem," he said, "Come with me." He installed me in a sound booth and handed me a record jacket, a Rod McKuen album with lyrics on the back. "Just read this into the mic. Dave through that window will signal you when to start." I had never been in a sound booth before and had never tried speaking into a microphone ... but I took a deep breath and spoke what was in front of me in the honeyed, hushed tone the words seemed to call for.

The next day I was offered a contract! I would be the voice for *Words and Music*, the station's new late-night show airing six times a week. I was excited to hear that I'd be able to choose all my own material – the pieces I would read – but had no idea at the time just what I was taking on. I've always loved poetry, and the thought of being able to share my many favourites this way sounded like a dream come true. But with two or sometimes three selections airing during each half hour segment, that meant finding ten poems or short prose readings every night ... or *sixty* a week! Week after week. To add to the challenge, only certain pieces would align with the intimate/smoky/sultry vibe they were looking to present. With child in tow and notebook handy, I began to haunt the library every afternoon searching for suitable material. Emily Dickinson to Shakespeare, Khalil Gibran to Shelley, Keats, and Browning, e.e. cummings,

Irving Layton, and Rod Stewart ... I would get happily lost in my research and learned more about poetry than I ever had before.

I was scheduled to come into the studio to record two mornings a week, with the pieces later being fitted into the nightly show. I had never been in front of a microphone before and picked up any technique on the job. Nor had I ever been in a sound booth – it all took some getting used to. The audio engineers across from me in the control room were patient and supportive as I worked to figure it all out during those first few weeks. They taught me about level checks and the trick to doing effective pick-ups when certain isolated lines had to be re-recorded if I flubbed a word or there was a technical glitch. I learned how to change the angle of my face in relation to the mic or turn slightly off-mic to prevent "popping" that can happen when breath hits the mic. Once they saw I felt more at home, they'd often come up with ways they thought would help me get into the mood for my sessions (which I'd record at 9 a.m. to be played all sexy and buttery-voiced at the midnight hour). I'd come into the booth where they had lowered the lights and placed some votives so I could lean in and read by candlelight. Or, looking up from my reading, I'd catch one or the other of the technicians unbuttoning his shirt and doing (his version of) a slow, steamy striptease! It kept things entertaining, but sometimes I had to focus *very* hard so I wouldn't dissolve into giggles in the middle of a particularly tender or wistful reading.

From the outset, it was agreed that I would not – *could* not – speak about my involvement in the show. The premise was that the person behind the voice had to be anonymous: a nameless, unidentifiable late-night "date" that could draw listeners in. Someone to connect with, who was talking only to them; the illusion of anonymity made it intimate. And it worked. Listeners were hooked and the show soon had a great following. One day as I arrived at the studio, the receptionist handed me a big packet of letters – actual fan mail! People wrote in and shared thoughts and longings, sent me their poems to consider reading, even asked if I was single and would I like to have dinner sometime? My husband knew about my work, of course, but was also sworn to secrecy. About twice a week, a group of his friends – fellow students – would be over at our place studying and working on assignments; invariably at 11:25 one of them would remind the group, "Better turn on the radio – almost time for *Words and Music*." I guess they thought it was soothing or sexy ... or something ... and they never knew the voice they were tuning in for came from someone doing crossword puzzles in the next room!

After I was there for a while, I started recording station IDs, program promos, show intros and outros, and 30-, 60-, and 90-second commercial spots. I became familiar with the built-in rhythm and unique tempo of advertising copy. I had practice pacing my delivery to get often way too many words into just the right number of seconds. It was kind of a crash course – I learned so much. I also had the fun of pushing my daughter through the mall in her stroller and hearing my voice over the PA system inviting shoppers to, "Have a beauty break this week at Poinciana Beauty Centre, 117 Lakeport Rd., at the end of Ontario Street... " – or some variation thereof. (Written across the top of this ad copy when I recorded was, "OD-1 / side 2 / cut 1 ... Pat, read quickly I can't cut anything out!")

Working at the station meant I also had lots of material for my voice tape, handy for approaching people who hired voice-over talent when I returned to Toronto.

And I returned soon, my marriage having collapsed one final time due to any number of stumbling blocks and differences of opinion about how we wanted to live our lives. Alcohol, pressures from work, and not being all on-board about what it meant to be parents, to be a family, real life stuff like that. My husband always maintained that it was unfair for me to ask him to make a choice between us and his "lifestyle." For me and our daughter, the lifestyle he chose over and over again brought only pain and heartbreak. And when he left, he *left*. The final curtain. No long goodbye. Never to see either of us for another fourteen years. Child support and alimony had always been things he mocked. So back I moved to Toronto, a sole-support parent with my adorable four-year-old. Broke and hustling. Time to start all over again.

I considered going back to teaching, but I knew that returning full time to the classroom plus caring for my daughter, would leave me without the hours or the energy to pursue acting or any involvement in theatre activity. I knew I'd miss it too much, so I decided to take part-time work teaching drama classes and look for openings wherever I could to stay on the scene. I needed to work *right* away … and the easiest, quickest opening was as a background actor – an extra – in the very busy film industry I found on my return to the city. With the help of some family nearby and childcare exchanges set up with friends who also had small children, I freed up time to book gigs on sets of locally produced films, big

American motion pictures, TV shows, videos and commercials.

Pay wasn't great, but work was plentiful. As part of the human scenery, I walked past buildings, through the airport, upstairs, downstairs, across a highway, along the canal; I sat at a bar, in a church congregation, at a hockey game, and a hospital emergency room. I danced at wedding receptions, a Bat Mitzvah, did line-dancing at a country and western bar, and was part of a pagan circle dance in a field at midnight. When I wasn't wearing my own clothes, Wardrobe dressed me as a nurse, a hippie, a federal judge, a pioneer woman, a vagrant, and a nun. In one episode of TV's crime drama *Night Heat* – due I guess to an oversight by the background casting agent – I was on camera as a uniformed police officer at the start of the show, then reappeared as a hooker being taken into custody, all black fishnets and satin miniskirt, during the second half hour!

Hours were long, lots of downtime waiting around, sometimes freezing on outdoor shoots all night. But I got to pay my bills, stay in touch with the industry, and get exposure to working on professional sets. I learned to listen to exactly what was required for a shot and to repeat it, sometimes ten or twelve times, as consistently as possible so continuity people wouldn't get bent out of shape. I came to understand the various shots and angles that made up a scene: the tightly-framed close up, the medium and long shot, the high angle and the low, the over-the-shoulder and the reverse shot. And the importance of eyeline – where an actor fixes their gaze – was a major take-away ... how maintaining proper eyeline and technically planning eyeline matches were crucial for an effective final product.

Being on set was also a way to meet other actors and creatives. Many singers, musicians, dancers, and between-engagement directors worked as background performers to fill gaps in their employment. There were the "professional extras," who saw this as a career, and weren't looking for anything more than being involved in creating a believable atmosphere or sense of reality for a film. And perhaps coming in contact with stars they admired, a little brush with celebrity. I heard many conversations on set that opened with something like, "I had a scene last week with Matt Damon. Yeah, walked right behind him and Ben Affleck. We were shooting at U of T ... of course it was supposed to be Harvard." (He had obviously been on the set of *Good Will Hunting* and I'm betting would have been first in line to catch the movie when it opened locally.) I heard over and over again that being an extra could be a career-killer. That directors and people with hiring ability viewed extras as "non-actors" and wouldn't consider them for lead or even speaking roles. Oh well, I thought, if they didn't have enough imagination to see past that, too bad for me; I needed to earn a living.

Getting to know other actors on set, I found a number of them were "union" performers. Their union was ACTRA, the Alliance of Canadian Cinema, Television, and Radio Artists. When I listened in on talk of meal penalties (when the first meal break didn't happen before the sixth hour of the filming day), compensation for travel time, and overtime pay scale if filming ran in excess of eight hours, and another rate if it was in excess of twelve hours, I thought I'd better find out more. Besides, people on set were always just *assuming*, and I often heard, "Well, you're ACTRA, right?" Because if you weren't, what was wrong with you? I think I may even have fibbed about this in the company of some pompous actors who obviously looked down on us, the pitiable unprotected masses.

I looked into how to become a member. At that time, you needed to land a role in a production under ACTRA jurisdiction. You couldn't get a union card without being offered a union gig, and you couldn't get a union gig until you were a member of the union. It was like the old riddle: which came first, the chicken or the egg? If the chicken didn't come first, where the heck did that egg come from? So it was a dilemma and a vexation. Later on, the system evolved so you could start as an apprentice if you were a recent film or theatre grad from accepted post-secondary institutions or amassed three qualifying credits in union productions, but you had to do this in a timely manner to avoid the hard-earned credits expiring. If you were a member in good standing of the sister-union, Actors Equity, representing performers in live theatre, a reciprocal agreement could get you in too. The joining process and paperwork were complicated, and it all seemed like a longshot for me at the time. But being an ACTRA member could open up opportunities, provide rights and protection, offer a safety net in terms of healthcare and pension benefits, and most of all, it seemed to confer validity, respectability. It announced you as a part of the established network and a contributor to its working order. So for years, union membership seemed like the pot of gold at the end of the rainbow.

It was something to strive for, an arduous challenge, especially trying to nab the kind of roles that qualified without an agent to get me into the audition room. And it was discouraging when speaking one line in a big American feature like *I'll Take Manhattan* resulted in a credit and working two seasons on an excellent show like *Degrassi Junior High* counted for nothing (in the early days, *Degrassi* had been contracted by CBC as an acquisition instead of a co-production with union requirements). It didn't seem to make sense. But I tried. And tried. I wanted to be *respectable*, of course I did! I was chasing after an idea of something I was convinced I needed. I felt if I could just push through, do all the things I was supposed to do, and ride the tide of circumstances and things I couldn't control, my determination would pay off.

When a good friend and I were both offered roles in a non-union production, she had to request permission to appear in the show as a "guest artist," because she was a union performer. For whatever reason, permission was denied. For me, that was a turning point. Looking back I thought of all the amazing adventures I had had doing non-union work, work I never even would have discovered if the union had anything to say about it. Strange and wonderful days, weeks, months on film sets and alternative theatre stages. And finally the danger – the *emptiness* - of hanging all my notions of success on some external benchmark became clear. Winning a union card was certainly an accepted "step up" as far as an acting career blueprint went. This was part of the culture I had absorbed.

Now suddenly I understood how being so focused on that end could kind of hem you in, and close you off from the chance to be … lucky! I had to weigh the risks and rewards of union membership. I also thought hard about the idea that if *no* actors were willing to do non-union jobs, producers would have to hire and work under union contracts ... did that mean that I was part of "pulling down" and harming the artistic community if I went indie? I struggled some with that. I realized how unquestioningly (and obsessively) I had been chasing the goal of union membership, and how it kept making me feel like I was coming up short. It was time to figure out what success as an actor looked like for *me*. So I decided: enough. I would go forward unprotected. I would be non-union. Hell ... I would be the QUEEN of non-union!

I kept doing background work, once in a while being upgraded to a "special business" extra, or getting a line here and there. I had lines and played small parts on various TV series shooting in Toronto. And I worked in a whole mittful of films for an independent company that kept churning them out at a staggering rate. It was a non-union operation producing low-budget 96-minute dramas – a lot of crime action/adventure, covering mafia-based drug smuggling, hijacking, cops gone bad, rackateers, and investigative thrillers. I played several detectives, lots of lawyers, a crime boss, an informant, and a madam in an after-hours joint or two. Shot mainly for television, I think, the films did have worldwide distribution. I know they were dubbed in many languages, likely a cheap product to sell abroad for countries looking for North American fare. I used to imagine stepping off a plane in places like Andorra or Comoros, Estonia or Guinnea-Bissau and being greeted by hordes of fans who knew me from these films. It tickled me to play that scene out in my head from time to time!

I was eager to get back to live theatre. Competition was fierce, the well-established theatres often cast from a smallish pool of talent, and even booking an audition for certain companies or productions felt like a major accomplishment for a non-union performer. Various actor-friends, tired of not being given the chance to audition for the roles they wanted, then tired of always waiting, trying *to be chosen*, decided to create their own opportunities. They would write and produce their own show! They could write different, better, *juicier* roles for themselves! This would give them more control: they could *work* instead of waiting around for work. It made sense, and as impressed as I was with their boldness and confidence, I never considered going that route. I guess I just wasn't that entrepreneurial. Plus I had no idea (and little interest in learning) about things like raising money, partnering with a venue, and marketing. But shows were produced. Some scripts were one person's vision, written individually, some evolved collaboratively. Quite a few found a home at the theatre "fringe" festival.

I got to work in fringe shows for a number of summers, and those are memories I'm glad I didn't miss out on. I've always loved the story of how fringing started. It was back in the 1940s in Scotland when some theatre types became discouraged and disillusioned with the theatre elitism they were experiencing. Shut out of the best playhouses, they decided to present their own shows in small, makeshift venues "around the fringes" of the grand Edinburgh International Arts Festival. The tradition spread, coming to Canada several decades later. The program is an eclectic mix of offerings: lots of original scripts (sometimes of questionable caliber), usually delivered by small casts and coming in somewhere around an hour in length. Some stuff is experimental, some racy, some site-specific. Participation is by open lottery, purportedly to give anyone and everyone a chance to share their vision and have their voice heard. 100% of ticket sales goes to the theatre company, with audience members encouraged to "tip the fringe" in order to keep the annual machine running.

Many lottery winners cast actor-friends in their shows, but I had to audition for my first fringe experience. I was cast in a two-hander, playing a ghost. Well, ghosts … plural – I think the thing that got me the part was being able to come up with five different voices/accents on the spot during the audition read. The playwright took the other role and we were directed by an eccentric Australian fellow who carried a pouch of brewer's yeast on his belt, which he'd sprinkle on the Big Macs he brought to rehearsal, announcing that they were now "health food." We worked like crazy promoting the show, throwing ourselves into the vibrancy that was the fringe, and actually made okay money. I was hooked, and looked forward to the following year's auditions … ready for round two. I missed out that time, but played in several more shows over the years – two original written-for-the-fringe efforts of dubious quality and an adaptation of Chekov's *The Marriage Proposal.*

As my daughter and I were alone together, I suppose it was natural that she was swept along into my pursuit of all things theatrical. I didn't always realize how much she was taking in or the effect my choice of career was having on her.

When a friend was in town doing a show, I decided to plan a day with my daughter – lunch out at our favourite restaurant, then off to see a matinée. Unfortunately I wasn't familiar with the play and didn't realize that that one of the characters was murdered at the end of the first act. I saw it coming and instantly regretted not having done some research before booking tickets. Too late, though: the deed happened on stage and my five-year-old took it very hard, very seriously. Intermission was spent trying to console her, explaining that it wasn't real, that no one had died, and that we'd see the actress later when the cast all came out to take a bow. Except, wouldn't you know it … no curtain call during this particular show. My daughter was distraught. I had to think fast. "The person you're worried about is an actor, just like me – she was playacting. If she really died, how would they be able to do the show tomorrow?" And then I learned just how much I had oversold my feelings about the competitive nature of the business: "Mommy, they could just get another girl! You always say actresses are a dime a dozen …"

My daughter lived with the reality of my job-to-job income, aware that I was always waiting for the phone to ring, to hear the results of an audition, to be hopefully snapped up for my next gig. And though she discovered at a young age that dance was where her heart was, she also determined that the vagaries of a performing life were not for her. People would ask, "So do you want to be on stage like your mom when you grow up?" My very practical daughter always answered the same way: "No, I want to have a lot of money. I'm going to be a dentist in the day and a dancer at night in my spare time."

Although I didn't teach my daughter to read super-early so she could run lines with me the way *my* mother had, I was lucky to have her as my accomplice in learning script after script, role after role. She knew how to skip ahead to pages where I had dialogue and when to hint at a line I had forgotten or correct me if I strayed too far from the text. When she was young, it was a fun activity to share; we'd sit down together with a big bowl of popcorn and laugh about the funny voices she'd use for the various characters she was reading. After she was about ten, I had to bribe her to help out. Then one day when I asked her to run lines, it was, "Mom, don't you realize I have a *life* now?" So that was it for my line-running-buddy-in-residence!

Five
SUMMER CAMP FOR ACTORS

Summer theatre - or the "straw-hat circuit," as it's known south of the border – always had a magical appeal for me. From the first time I heard of these playhouses, often located near resort or vacation areas, that offered summer-long entertainment ... AND work for actors – I wanted *in*. (Okay, those old Mickey Rooney-let's-find-a-barn-and-put-on-a-show movies didn't hurt either.) It sounded like the perfect working vacation or maybe "summer camp" for actors! Turns out, it's a little bit of both. And a whole lot more.

When a friend started talking about having to sublet his apartment for a couple of months, and another actor-friend asked if I was interested in boarding Keltie, her little terrier, for the last two weeks in July and all of August, I knew this was my cue. I bombarded them with questions. Both were heading to different summer theatres that they had worked at before. Of course contracts had all been signed and casting completed for that season, but I determined to submit photos, resumés, and whatever else was necessary to try to snag an audition for the following summer. I would make this happen! And I did. In January the theatres announced their seasons, and I considered which ones were planning shows I might be right for. Some did exclusively musicals (which let me out, as I wasn't a singer or one of those triple-threat performers), there were lots of comedies, and various plays with regional themes, possibly new works reflecting the rural or Canadian perspective. I ended up reading for several directors, and – oh, happy day! – I got cast in *Brighton Beach Memoirs*, my first summer theatre gig.

I was beside myself with excitement, all nervous energy and giddy anticipation. What would it be like? Where would I be living? Who were the other actors and the people I'd be working with? Would they like me? Would I like them? *Could I do this*? And it would be months before any of these questions would be answered! I tried to pull off being low-key about my summer gig as I carried on with my normal activities of teaching, auditioning, caring for my daughter, paying the bills, seeing friends and family. I'm not sure why I felt I needed to seem blasé about it, maybe because so many of the actors I knew had been doing this for years and were accustomed to zipping away to work here and there. They seemed further along in their careers; comparison is a fool's game and I felt like I was always playing catch-up.

When mid-July came, I was off to the Lake Erie Summer Playhouse for six weeks! All the actors would be living together in a huge house on the lake, rented just for them, within walking distance of the theatre. Often for summer theatre work, actors and crew members from out of town are billeted with local residents who open their homes for a month or two. Local people get to be involved in supporting theatre, and may receive tax receipts, season's tickets to shows, or gift cards to exchange at local businesses. For many who do it year after year, it's an enjoyable change and fresh company they look forward to. Some cook for you, enjoy hearing all the gossip at the end of the day, some take a more arms-length approach to hosting the performers. Some billeting hosts have strict rules about storing and labelling food in the refrigerator or when the air conditioner can be turned on, some neglect to disclose they smoke in the house and occasion hasty relocation challenges for an allergic actor, some allow you to bring a pet along ... or expect you to walk their giant Great Dane before you turn in at the end of a long day. I've had various experiences being billeted with local townsfolk through the years but I'm glad my first summer theatre gig didn't involve this arrangement: I had enough I was feeling uncertain about.

We performed in a heritage building, a stately space, that had housed some kind of municipal offices in a former lifetime. It's part of a sprawling southern Ontario network of historic buildings – warehouses, firehalls, churches, and other unused venues – renovated and re-purposed into settings for theatrical activity. There's the Arts Barn near Bobcaygeon, once a working cattle barn, Port Stanley's Town Hall Theatre, and the Upper Canada Playhouse in Morrisburg, formerly the Toothbrush and Argyle Sock Factory. And many more, some of which I've had the pleasure and good fortune to have played in over many summers.

The summer theatre business attracts tourists to the townships. It's good for the local economy, with restaurants, shops, inns and short-term rentals benefiting from a shot in the arm they can count on every year. Along with that is the infusion of energy, the excitement of change that comes from having new people and new elements as part of the local community for a time. Each place I've worked has seemed to embrace the actors and their seasonal theatre activity. Residents stop you on the street to say how much they enjoyed the show, shopkeepers recognize you, the server at the donut shop knows how you take your coffee. And actors get to insert themselves into the local scene at whatever level they're comfortable with. I'll never forget patting Gilda, the miniature donkey, at a county fair before a Saturday matinée, and I still set my table with the four pistol-handled knives I bought at Hudson's Antiques another summer. The pop-up guest teaching I was invited to do for a day camp improv class remains a highlight. Living and working for a while in the community, you feel more like a local than a tourist.

But make no mistake: there's a *lot* of work to be done! In a short time. Pulling a show together so it's ready for an audience in one to two weeks - ten days is fairly common – is a big process. Directors, designers, and technical staff have made initial decisions before arriving. Actors are generally expected to know their lines so rehearsals can focus on things like timelines and the stage picture. Memorizing lines is simple, concrete preparation an actor can do alone that helps them be ready for direction, blocking, and characters' reactions to each other once the company comes together. Just one actor who isn't off-book or close to it at the outset can really slow progress and frustrate the heck out of the director and other cast members.

Rehearsals are intense and can mean working long hours. It's often necessary to rehearse shows out of sequence, or to run scenes off-site, not having a chance to work on stage until just before opening night. Through it all, actors are under pressure to remember all the notes and changes the director wants, as well as deal with sets, lighting, sound, and costuming as they're brought on board. If shows are running in rep – an actor may be in productions running simultaneously or on alternating weeks – there's the added stress of memorizing multiple scripts and having different directors to please. My favourite thing, though, about doing a summer theatre show is that it's almost like being on another planet or some kind of remote island. You're isolated, "real life" with all its usual day-to-day concerns is on pause. Focus becomes easier. There's just you, the other actors, and the work.

Pages from my rehearsal log – ten days getting a show ready for our audience – offers a peek into the process

Rehearsal log: *Rumors* by Neil Simon,
Beaverton Summer Arts Festival

Monday, day 1
First rehearsal called for 10 a.m. Introductions are made as actors arrive at the theatre in the Old Town Hall. Some of the players have been colleagues before; some have worked with this director on other productions. The director welcomes everyone, and distributes rehearsal schedules. Morning (10 – 1 p.m.), afternoon (2 – 6), and evening sessions (7 – 10) have been mapped out so we can accomplish everything in ten days. Building the set started the day before, and structurally it's almost complete. An area on the floor is paced out and taped to

represent the set; it's here that the actors will work until construction is finished. All day is spent blocking Act 1: entrances, exits, and general traffic control are the director's concerns at this stage of the game. In this play, with sometimes all ten characters on stage at once, this is a challenge! After a full day of work, it's back to the house that's been rented for the company's stay. It's a large, wood-paneled cottage with a laundry room, sundeck, huge backyard, and steps leading down to the beach. A beach! Actors come home to a wonderful dinner of pasta, salad, and crusty bread, prepared by a couple of the cast members. Different people, or groups of people, it's been decided (??), will take turns providing dinner each night for the bunch of us. Lots of talk and merriment around the table as actors trade stories and get to know each other.

Tuesday, day 2
Before rehearsal this morning, the women go for costume try-ons. The local person in charge of wardrobe has gathered potential costumes and now fit and appropriateness must be determined. Two of the four women find something suitable; more stuff will be rounded up. To begin rehearsal, the director gives an informal talk on farce – the concept and how it differs from playing other types of comedy. Some of the actors have not done farce before, others have had lots of experience with the genre. All get a kick out of the director's descriptions of their roles as "stock" characters: the one-dimensional buffoon, the senile old fool, the pragmatic airhead, etc. Act 1 is run, and it's declared a productive morning. After lunch, we begin blocking Act 2. During the late afternoon, the screech of the circular

saw and the whir of the electric drill on stage become a challenge (good exercise in focus and voice projection for the actors!) The evening's rehearsal is moved to one of the council rooms downstairs so noise won't be a distraction. A "stage" is set up, rehearsal begins, but fifteen minutes later we learn that the room is required for town business, and actors troop upstairs again. The noise is a big hurdle, but all of Act 2 gets blocked. We meet the last two actors who've just arrived today, so now our cast is complete. Everyone's exhausted – dinner and beverages back at the house, and an early night.

Wednesday, day 3
Today we get to work on stage for the first time. Structurally, the set is almost complete – only the upper level can't be used yet, as the landing isn't deemed secure and there are no railings. So now the stage, which has been in total disarray until today, looks very orderly, almost bare. The rest of the theatre, on the other hand, is a fascinating hodge-podge – cluttered with lumber, ladders, tools, tables, chairs, props and furniture ... including a dentist's chair used in the last show, *Little Shop of Horrors*. The area is strewn with an assortment of every type of bottled water, constant companion of the actor in rehearsal. (The IGA across the street has its own "Our Compliments" brand on special at 99 cents for a 1.5 litre bottle, and this seems to be the favourite today.) The men are called away to try on tuxedos, shirts, and cummerbunds when they're not needed on stage. Morning and afternoon sessions are spent working Act 1. In the evening the set painters are at work, so it's back to the taped area on the floor for the actors. At 9:30 everyone is released except the six actors who will appear in the short dance sequence. The

director plays the music that we'll use – Hot, Hot, Hot! – and tells us that the dance sequence will be very tightly choreographed. And that she's going to teach it to us NOW. Wails and moans of "Why can't we just freeform?" are ignored, and the lesson begins. Most of the actors are not used to picking up choreographed routines, and it's tough going. And frustrating. And *hilarious!* After lots of laughter – and more moaning – the director dismisses the actors and tells them they've earned a good night's sleep.

Thursday, day 4
Lots of painting has been done on the set by the time we arrive this morning – the base coat has been applied and everything looks very white. The railing for the stairs and second-floor landing are now in place. This is the day in the schedule when actors are supposed to be "off book." The director is very supportive, says she's aware it will be a struggle, but reminds everyone that it's a necessary part of the process. Actors all know this; they're at various stages of committing lines to memory, and know how insecure they'll feel for the first time without a script in hand. It *is* a struggle, and the assistant director is kept busy calling out missed or mangled lines or forgotten blocking. Morning session ends with eight run-throughs of the dance sequence. "Not bad!" says the director, and we try to believe her. After lunch painting resumes on set so we're back to rehearsing on the floor. This evening, for the first time, we run the show from top to bottom. This is important so everyone can begin to feel the flow of the action. First act not too bad, second act long and slow. But we muddle through.

Friday, day 5
We see the colour of the walls on our set when we arrive at the theatre: a rich-looking pale butterscotch – it looks great. We run Act 1 and various bits all morning and give Act 2 the same treatment in the afternoon. A fabulous dinner (homemade pizza, zesty salad, and an unbelievable dessert dubbed "Vergie's Chocolate Almond Ecstasy") puts everyone in a happy, if somewhat lethargic, mood. Rehearsal is at the house tonight as the theatre has been taken over by a touring production of *Godspell*. A line run is deemed the most efficient use of time in this space, so we sit around the living room bashing out the lines. The stage manager is furiously marking his script with big Xs each time a line is missed or mangled. Energy is dropping towards the end of the second act, and silliness sets in. The director tries to keep everyone focused and on track, but gives up at 10 o'clock and releases everyone except the dancers. We work the routine half a dozen times. Still lots of moaning and groaning.

Saturday, day 6
Today is a day for running both acts, then working bits that have been identified as troublesome by either the director or the actors. As scenes are worked on stage, small groupings of players are scattered about the theatre running lines with each other. Tonight we rehearse in a nearby church, as there's a function at the theatre again. It's a satisfying session, and everyone leaves feeling encouraged about several scenes that are finally coming together.

Sunday, day 7
Actors have the morning off as technical staff work out

lighting and sound cues. We're called for 2 p.m., but don't get to use the stage until 3:30. Then there's only time for a technical cue-to-cue before dinner break, which comes very late anyway. Actors wander around town trying to find a restaurant that's open Sunday night. Most finally settle for take-out Reddi-Chef, and eat their chicken hurriedly at the picnic tables behind the theatre. Then we do a bit more cue-to-cue stuff, work a couple of scenes in Act 2, and call it a night.

Monday, day 8
Scenic trim on the set is being finished as scenes are worked on stage this morning, and actors are disconcerted at times to be doing business – maybe making drinks at the bar – and to look down and see someone lying on the floor at their feet *painting.* Good exercise in focus and concentration! The scenic designer – who is also one of the actors – is "forging" art masterpieces to hang on the set walls. He works studiously from pictures in several big art books; at the moment the Piet Mondrian book is open at page 91, "Composition." After dinner, technical dress rehearsal. Tech stuff not too bad, but there is general fluster among the players as they cope with costumes and actual props for the first time.

Tuesday, day 9
Actors a little down this morning after last night. Director tells us not to panic, pointing out that we still have 20% of our prep time ahead of us: a helpful perspective – two out of ten days of rehearsal left – none of us had thought of it that way. Painters are still busy on stage as scenes are being worked. After lunch break, the sofas are carried upstairs into the theatre and set on stage. The cast has

been anxious for their arrival as it's suspected size and shape may mean modifications to blocking. Full technical dress rehearsal tonight. The temperature is 33 degrees … backstage and on stage under the lights it feels like an *oven*. Sweat glistens on every brow (except Roz's – what's her secret?) Actors commiserate, fanning themselves furiously with any available prop each time they make an exit. Director is pleased. Everyone leaves feeling encouraged by tonight's run … and fairly optimistic about tomorrow's preview.

<u>Wednesday, day 10</u>
Cast has the morning off. Some actors sleep 'till noon, some enjoy a leisurely breakfast in town and wander down to the lakeside to run lines, some do errands or go for a swim. Director and scenic designer finish painting the set, while the stage manager tacks down the sisal carpet on stage so actors don't trip and add unintended pratfalls to the show. During the afternoon, a line run is organized at the picnic tables. A slight interruption as news comes downstairs that the stage manager has cut his hand badly on a broken plate used in the show. The producer is rounded up to drive him to the nearest hospital, where he gets a number of stitches. As tonight is a preview, and actors haven't seen much advertising, they're curious about whether they'll have an audience. No one seems to know. Dinner break, then back to the theatre for our first chance to try the show out in front of the public (maybe). Lots of nervous energy backstage. Then it's 8:10 and "Places!" are called. The new opening, rehearsed only half an hour ago, does not happen. Apart from that, things go not too badly and disasters are minor: a broken shoe strap, several muddled and/or

late sound cues, bits of mangled text or messy business here and there. Only a few dozen people see tonight's performance, but they are entertained. The director is less effusive with her praise tonight, but knows that as the actors relax into the run and enjoy hearty laughter from a full house, they will have a show. And so the players retire to study the (copious) helpful notes from the director, and to rest and dream of tomorrow's opening. The summer theatre experience ... ah, showbiz!

Six
WAS THIS IN MY PLAN?
(was I supposed to have a plan?)

When a long-running dinner theatre show closed, a cast member mentioned some work to me that he thought might be of interest. He said it was something he had been involved in for a few years: "It's interesting and it's *gold* for when you're between jobs. You can pick up shifts whenever you're free. A lot of actors do it." Catering? Market Research? Phone Sex? I didn't know what he was about to suggest, and even after he told me, I had no idea what he was talking about. He said he worked as a "standardized patient" - a medical actor - and asked me if I had ever seen the *Seinfeld* episode where Kramer got a job doing this work. I said I hadn't, then we got pulled into another conversation, and I forgot the whole thing. A month later, waiting for the phone to ring and wondering if I'd ever work again, I caught a late-night rerun of the Seinfeld episode.

Called "The Burning," it unspooled the story of Cosmo Kramer's gig where he was hired to portray someone with gonorrhea, which medical school students were tasked with diagnosing. He pulls out all stops as he performs for the doctors-in-training: dimmed lights, a maroon smoking jacket, a lit cigarette, his tale of a romantic evening, and "haunting memories of lost love." The students make the correct diagnosis, the doctor in charge applauds the performance, and Kramer is left wondering if he'll be forever typecast as "the gonorrhea patient." The comic genius of actor Michael Richards and the physical quirkiness he bestows on Kramer make the episode hilarious. I laughed out loud. Surely this couldn't be the work my friend had talked about?

But it was. I learned that though the episode was a wildly inaccurate depiction of what a medical actor does, it had its basis in truth. Sometimes called standardized patients, sample patients, or simulators, these people are hired to recreate medical scenarios so student doctors and other healthcare professionals can practice dealing with their future real-life patients. Doctors-in-training, nurses, pharmacists, physiotherapists, dentists, dieticians and more, engage in role-play with actors to try out techniques they're learning in lectures and labs. The theoretical becomes real. Sounded like an amazing way to use my skill set as an actor. I wanted in.

I found out about the application process for a program at the university, filled out forms and booked an interview. And after a brief orientation/training session, I was in. My friend had been right: "A lot of actors do it." About two-thirds of the simulators were actors, and anyone who came to the work without that background got a kind of crash course in Applied Theatre 101. It didn't take long to realize that I'd get to use and hone all my skills as an actor: learning and retaining information, memorization, listening and reacting, improvisation, creating a character, portraying consistently, taking direction, working collaboratively – phew! It would just be in a different arena. Instead of sharing a character on a theatre stage in front of a full house of ticket-holders, medical actors bring patients to life for a small, exclusive audience of two or six or as many as (gasp!) forty as part of a workshop or lecture.

  Not only did I get to use my skill set, I got to grow it. Realistically portraying things like fatigue, hyperactivity, lightheadedness, joint stiffness, numbness in hands or feet, or the deep, excruciating ache associated with cellulitis took some practice. I learned the various ways to show pain and the degree of discomfort. It might be tension in the way a certain part of the body is held, perhaps it's an occasional wince or a constant grimace. Maybe I'd be moaning as I lay curled up in a fetal position. (Thank you, theatre training: sense memory and imagination to the rescue!) I now can claim various types of abnormal breathing to "special skills" on my resumé – not that I'll probably ever get to use them in regular acting gigs. Things like tachypnea (rapid breathing), bradypnea (very slow), Cheyne-Stokes (cycle of shallow to deep breaths and back down again, followed by a brief period of apnea, or no breathing), apneustic (gasping on the inhale, a pause, then a short partial exhale), and Kussmaul (deep and rapid breathing) … all part of my wheelhouse now. And I mastered the "death rattle," an awful name for breathing often heard in terminal patients just before they die. A kind of wet respiration as people are no longer able to swallow, it's a pretty chilling sound. Playing the high affect roles made great use of acting skills: it might mean reacting to hearing bad news, a heavy diagnosis, maybe crying or raging, hallucinating, being delirious, violent or terrified. The patient may be at the end of life for one reason or another. These roles call for intense intellectual, emotional, and physical involvement.

The chance to bring some of these patient roles and medical scenarios to life through film and video projects became a fascinating part of the deal. Video tutorials and online learning was more effective than textbook descriptions for teaching physical maneuvers like applying bandages and splints or performing a respiratory or cardiac exam. And the visual and emotional engagement the media provided made it a great platform for conveying ideas about communication, ethics, attitudes, and professional behaviour. Some productions were simple and largely improvised; other videos were tightly-scripted, involving large casts, and a complete lighting, audio, and camera crew. I wasn't limited to playing a patient; I've been cast as a family member, a nurse (jaded, cranky), a pharmacist, a social worker, a doctor (who's having a dilemma about reporting a colleague), and a very judge-y medical receptionist. Often the cast would be a mix of actors and real healthcare providers. Of course the medical professionals brought life experience and authenticity to their roles, but were not always familiar or comfortable with some of the realities of filming. Camera angles, close-ups, technical considerations, and the multiple "takes" often necessary to capture what's needed was totally new to them. And as they weren't used to memorizing pages and pages of dialogue, the director often had to take a looser approach with the script. Actors had to be ready to roll with whatever lines and cues happened or didn't happen, as long as the story got told. Some doctors and nurses really enjoyed the process, perhaps "catching the bug" and discovering an unexpected acting talent. Inevitably, though, they needed to be reminded not to look at the camera when the director called "Action!"

Arriving back in the city from doing a show out of town, I found a message on my answering machine: a possible audition for *The Mousetrap.* The Agatha Christie thriller had been playing for a couple of decades at Toronto Truck Theatre, and had the distinction of being the longest running non-musical theatrical production in North America. Over the years, several friends had done the show, some for months, some for a couple of years, and I had been to the intimate and charming theatre on Belmont Street to see them play on various occasions. Invariably they'd mention that I should really come out to audition the next time there was a role that needed to be filled. The cast was always in flux, they added, and they could let me know when there might be an opening for a new actor. For some reason, I always pooh-poohed the idea, thinking, "Why on earth would I want to do the same show over and over again, maybe *forever*?" So I never submitted my photo and resumé, and have no idea how the audition invitation came to be on my answering machine.

Without any other immediate prospects for work, I considered that maybe the chance for solid, ongoing employment on stage might not be something to turn my nose up at. I knew from newspaper ads that there were eight shows a week, and with the theatre within walking distance from my apartment, suddenly the idea started to seem more unappealing. I dialed the call-back number and set up an appointment. And the next week and a half went like this:

<u>Wednesday</u>
My audition appointment this afternoon with Juraj Politzer, currently in charge of directing *The Mousetrap*. They're looking for an understudy for the role of Mrs. Boyle. Mr. Politzer meets me at the theatre door; he's charming and professional, we chat a bit, then I go up on stage to do my monologue. He's asked for something in a British accent as that's what's required for the show. He thanks me and hands me a photocopied scene from the play to take home and look over for a second audition sometime during the next week. But – hurray! – later that day Mr. Politzer calls to say he doesn't need to hear me again, that he's comfortable offering me the understudy role for Mrs. Boyle. He tells me that rehearsing the show will be unlike anything I've experienced before. This sounds intriguing! He explains that rehearsing will be accomplished scene by scene, in little bits. Then ... can I come to see the show tomorrow night to write down my character's blocking? Uh, okay ... I guess I'm in.

<u>Thursday</u>
I arrive at the theatre just as they're opening the house, and slip into the back row (which turns out not to be the ideal spot from which to scribble down blocking notes into my script – not enough light, should've sat three rows forward). Waiting for the show to begin, I notice a fellow alone, sitting right in front of me, script in hand. I wonder if he's there for the same reason I am? I say hi and find out that Bingo! ... he *is* – he's Jason, and he'll soon be taking over the role of Giles Ralston. He tells me this is his third time out to write down the blocking. The director had told me to come downstairs and introduce myself to the cast after the first act. I worry that this might be sort

of peculiar – annoying – as actors are in the middle of the show and all. Turns out Jason is thinking the same thing, but he says he'll go if I do. The director meets us downstairs as we slip behind the makeshift partition to the dressing room area and introduces us to everybody on their intermission break. My first rehearsal is set for the next day before the show!

Friday
My first rehearsal on stage tonight, scheduled from 7pm until about 7:40. Unusual, but one assumes an efficient timeslot, so the current cast are not required to be at the theatre when they wouldn't already be there anyway. We're rehearsing the scene between my character and Miss Casewell, played tonight by Betsy Palmerston (although I note that in the show I attended last night, she played Mrs. Boyle). The director talks me through the action of the short scene, then we run it numerous times. He knows what he wants, and I work to incorporate his directives of "harsher"…"louder"…"Remember these are two strong women." There's a sound cue involved, and Phil up in the booth runs that a number of times so I can get used to it. Soon tonight's players must go to dress and prepare, so we're finished for now. I ask if I can stay and watch the first act again tonight. "That'll be twenty dollars!" jokes the director.

Saturday
Director has asked if I'm free during the day, and as I am, we arrange to meet at noon to do some work. He talks about the flow of the action and how my character fits in, animatedly sketching in his parameters for the role. "But," he says, "You create your own Boyle. You'll find your own

way. That's what makes it interesting." We go through several scenes. I have to work on my walk: "You walk lightly, like a young woman. Next time try to bring shoes for Mrs. Boyle – comfortable, sturdy – that will help." I make a note to pop around to the thrift shop in the next day or two to hunt for footwear. We discuss the murder scene. The director describes what's required, how I'll be the only character on stage and how it will be my job to create tension and fear for the audience. (I've died on stage before, but never been murdered … hope I can do this properly.) Not infrequently, ideas are conveyed in film terms: the medium shot, the close-up, and so forth, and it doesn't surprise me to learn later of my director's hefty background in film and television. Having worked dozens of new cast members into the various roles over the years, Juraj has thought through every line, every move, and by now could probably do this on automatic. But it never feels that way; he's patient and encouraging. Back at the theatre tonight before the show to work on a scene with Major Metcalf.

Sunday
Off to the thrift store this morning to search for shoes-that-make-me-walk-like-Mrs.-Boyle. The perfect brown lace-up shoes are there waiting for me! They fit, feel just right, and are mine for only $5.99. Heady with success, I cruise the aisles looking for a suit in earth tones that'll go with my new sensible shoes. I try on several and leave with a tweedy number that I'll be able to pull together accessories for another time.

Monday
Rehearsal tonight is called for 6:45 instead of the usual

7:00, as the group scene to be worked is more complex and involves the whole cast. It's for the benefit of three of us who will come aboard shortly. Jason (who I met the other night) will play Giles, Jeff starts as Christopher Wren in a week, and me. We run the entire scene several times, then go over bits with specific characters. One cast member offers to read in the part of Paravicini so Juraj, whose role that usually is, can put on his director's cap, stand back, and watch the action on stage. Second time through, this actor taking over requests – and receives – permission to "do the accent." He gives a very credible study of Juraj's roguish Eastern European intonation and speech patterns – everyone enjoys this! 7:40 comes quickly, and the stage manager announces that he'll open the house in five minutes. Actors are released to prepare for their show.

Tuesday
Tonight's rehearsal is mainly for Christopher Wren, but I've been asked to come along to go over the few lines when my character first meets Wren. I quickly learn the lines for that bit so all can run smoothly and my presence can be useful. I feel I have the lines down perfectly, but then … suddenly we're doing another scene we haven't gone through yet, one that I've barely looked at. Not sure if it's the out-of-sequence rehearsal style or what, but for some reason practically no lines seem to stick when I'm on stage. I feel a bit like an idiot. Like I'm holding everyone back. Finally Juraj hands me my script to read from and tells me not to worry. But I *do*; I vow to devote all day tomorrow to learning lines. (Jeff is splendid as Wren, though. My shoes work too!)

Wednesday
Director had explained that we'd leave my entrance scene until near the end of our rehearsal time. Tonight's the night. "Very important," he reiterates, "Very important to establish Boyle's character … as soon as you walk on stage, the audience must see that this is not a nice woman." I get to use coat, hat, scarf, and purse this time through and this helps a lot. I learn where the doorbell is offstage and exactly what my cue is for ringing it. We begin to rehearse the bit where I enter for the first time – Giles is the only other character required on stage with me for this. Soon the actress playing Mollie arrives and we get to carry the action a little further. The actor playing Giles in tonight's show switches and sportingly "becomes" Christopher Wren when he's needed, and a Metcalf I've never met is now walking on stage, so we run the complete scene two more times. We work to nail down the look Mrs. Boyle gives Giles as she exits upstairs. Then we jump to the murder scene that ends Act 1: Mollie discovers Mrs. Boyle's body on the couch, pushes her over, and screams. I get to practice my route for slipping offstage quickly and seamlessly in the blackout. For tonight, though, we just try it with the lights on.

Thursday
I'm excited as I arrive at the theatre. After rehearsal I'll get to stay for the show and shadow the actress who's playing Mrs. Boyle. All understudies shadow, a necessary step so they can get a solid grasp on the flow of the action: the only complete run-through they'll have is the first time they get to play in front of an audience. I wear my suit, shoes, hairnet – the whole get-up – for rehearsal to make sure it passes Juraj's inspection. He

approves of the suit, says he likes the transformation. We run the murder scene a couple of times. Juraj fine tunes some critical moves, and Doug up in the booth provides light and sound cues so I'll know how things will go. "So," says Juraj, "You are staying to shadow this evening, yes? And then you will be ready." I go downstairs and tonight's Mrs. Boyle shows me around – where the various costume pieces hang, which space at the dressing room table will be mine, etc. Then the show is UP, and I sort of slink around behind the actress playing the part I'll be playing soon. I need to see exactly where and when entrances and exits happen, to discover little tasks I'll be responsible for – being handed and hanging up a coat offstage here, switching off a light there. I'm concerned about being in the way in the tiny, cramped wing space, but everyone seems comfortable with the process and is very helpful. Studying the show from this vantage point is fascinating – one usually doesn't have this opportunity except while waiting for a cue to enter the action on stage. But tonight, without the stress of a performance to give, I find this fly-on-the-wall perspective quite thrilling. An even bigger thrill comes minutes after Boyle makes her final exit and asks, "So how would you feel about doing the two shows this Saturday?"

What the director had told me when I accepted the gig was all true: rehearsals *were* like nothing I had ever experienced before! There we were, a week of rehearsing various bits and scenes on stage just before showtime for the regular cast. I learned that it hadn't always been this way – at one time, understudy and new-cast member rehearsals were held on Monday nights, traditionally when theatres were dark and there wasn't a show on stage. But with people in flux for many years and understudies and replacements having to constantly be rehearsed into the various roles, it seemed more efficient to accomplish this in small pieces, without requiring actors already in the show to be at the theatre on what would be their only night off. So those thirty to forty minutes just before players had to go and prepare for their audience was it.

My first night performing was pretty terrifying. Never having had a chance to stick those bits together, to run through the whole show, made it a moment-to-moment challenge. Cast members were used to suddenly having new actors dropped into the mix and were very helpful; I appreciated being gently moved into the proper spot at times and receiving "eye prompts" letting me know, "Okay, time for your line, Mrs. Boyle!" And to make it even trickier, some of the people I was on stage with that night hadn't been the ones I rehearsed with. They were actors I had never heard speaking those lines, players I had only met half an hour ago in the dressing room. This was something I would come to regard as normal.

As *The Mousetrap* had already been running for twenty-four years at this theatre, actors were always coming and going. Some would leave the show and come back to join the cast again years later, some took a month-long break to do other theatre work, others just needed a night or two off for family obligations or their own well-being and would call on their understudies to take over. I think I was there for about half a year before I stopped being surprised by who I might be on stage with on any particular night. It kept you on your toes, of course, because while the blocking was set and common, as it had to be to accommodate frequent cast changes, each new player brought something of their own to the show. Maybe a short, dramatic pause here, a more ironic line-reading there, a generally warmer or colder or more threatening tone throughout. Various cast members had learned a second, third, or even fourth role and would step in to play different characters on different nights. When replacements had to happen, it made sense to invite those already familiar with the show and the characters to learn another role – suddenly the in-house talent bank was increased. And it gave actors who might be intrigued by another of the roles a chance to try something new and grow their skills. But sometimes it was disconcerting to hear a voice behind you saying Miss Casewell's lines when the night before you knew that voice belonged to Mollie Ralston!

It was interesting having the director also playing one of the characters in the show. I had found him patient and thorough as a director, and instantly admired his work on stage as we played together. It was obvious that he delighted in playing Paravicini, who he described as the ultimate con artist, "an absolute and complete fake." He even hoped to seduce the audience, from the start, into wondering if perhaps his roguish Eastern European accent was put on, and that he was really British, hiding something by this manner of speaking. I was very aware that at times during a performance he would be watching actors as other characters in the unfolding drama and at times through his director's eyes. This could be disconcerting, especially when he was watching *me*. I always knew, just through a look, when I could expect a note after the performance. Uh oh, something was not *quite* right or needed to be tweaked "just a little." Perhaps a glance backwards to be added or a pointed upward inflection at the end of a line. I valued the input as I knew it would help me to polish my performance, but it still unnerved me sometimes to be caught in that director's gaze during a show.

Not all cast members seemed equally responsive to Juraj's feedback. Some had been doing the show for *years* and felt that they had their characters and various aspects of playing all figured out by this time. One danger of acting in a long-running production like *The Mousetrap* is that it's easy to slip into doing things on automatic; out of respect for his craft and the show, Juraj tried to stay on top of that. When he attempted to clean up any laziness or cutting corners that might have crept in, it was not always appreciated. And of course, as he was on stage with the rest of the players every night in addition to being the director, some actors were not amenable to being directed by their cast-mate. He saw that some people had trouble accepting notes after a show, either getting offended or constantly having excuses. Eventually he stopped giving notes to those actors, in hopes of keeping things on an even keel backstage.

The director was meticulous about keeping the stage picture just right. He liked to cast people of roughly the same height – no one very short or extra-tall – so the difference wouldn't be a distraction for the audience. And while actors could contribute suggestions about how their characters might dress, Juraj had well thought-out and very firm ideas about appearance, costuming, even hair styles. He insisted on an upswept bun-type hairdo for the women. I do recall the very few occasions when Juraj had a night off and the actress playing Mollie took advantage of his absence to forego the bobby pins, shake out her locks, and share a more "let your hair down" mistress of Monkswell Manor with the audience!

Playing the grumpy, older Mrs. Boyle, I wore a hairnet to keep my curly blond hair looking appropriately uptight. I went through several hairnets a week, and suddenly could no longer find the colour I always bought at the drug store. Or anywhere else. So I wrote to Goody, the manufacturer, asking what had happened, and explaining how important the hairnets were to my portrayal on stage. They must have taken me seriously because I soon received a letter back from the Merchandising Specialist. They said they had done some colour analysis and discovered that their supplier had changed up the colours a bit, but that it would be corrected. A complimentary box containing *hundreds* of hairnets in the colour I needed was delivered with the letter, which ended ...

"Please find enclosed some replacement hairnets in the light colour #024J. We can't have the Canadian theatre scene in jeopardy. We understand that Mrs. Boyle must look like a stern, crotchety older woman. You keep up the good work with the changes in your voice, mannerisms, and movement, and Goody will look after your hair."

Responsive *and* a sense of humour! The letter went up on a bulletin board backstage, and made me smile every time I saw it.

I originally joined the company as an understudy, but the main cast actor was going through personal problems and immediately began handing over almost all her shows to me. Understudies never had their names in the program; lobby cards, changed before each show, announced any casting changes: "In tonight's performance, the role of Major Metcalf (or Christopher Wren or Mollie Ralston, etc.) will be played by _____." But once it became clear that I was there for eight shows a week, and had been for months and months, my bio was added to the program as the official Mrs. Boyle. And that's how it remained until the show closed almost two years later.

About a year into doing the show, I took some time off to travel to England, and the possibility of seeing *The Mousetrap* on the London stage excited me. It had been playing in the West End for almost half a century, setting all kinds of "longest-running" records. A formidable production, I imagined, in the place where it originated, and one that had boasted many respected members of the British theatre scene, including celebrated players such as Richard Attenborough, Patrick Stewart, and Julie Walters in the roles through the years. I hadn't entirely decided I *wanted* to add it to my must-see list of shows while in London. How would it make me feel about our show? Would the scale and reputation of the production overwhelm me and make me question what we were doing? Would my take-away be, "Ah, *this* is how it's supposed to be done"? My curiosity won out, though, and I was off one evening to St. Martin's Theatre. And thanks to a friendly chat at the box office, where I shared that I was involved in the Canadian production, I got to watch from my own private booth (which the box office knew was not booked that evening) and for free! I was mesmerized, drawn in – I loved watching the story and characters from this fresh perspective: familiar and known, but NEW at the same time. I couldn't believe I almost passed on the chance to see the show. I came home feeling good about what we were doing in our little, much-less-opulent playhouse, telling the story of those gathered at Monkswell Manor trying to discover the murderer in their midst. Bonus!

News that our Toronto show would close after running for twenty-six and a half years came as a shock to the cast. The producer's decision to shut the show down was influenced (hastened?) by the fact that houses had started to dwindle, royalty payments became harder and harder to keep up with, and the theatre stood on prime, prized real estate. Maybe we should have seen the writing on the wall. Although the decision must have been made months earlier, cast and company members were advised five weeks before the date of the final show. Most of us heard the news over the phone and were unprepared for that jolt of reality. I had been doing the show for two years, and for some it was lots longer, eight years' livelihood for one of my cast-mates.

The final performance was a gala affair, by invitation only. All former cast members who could be contacted were invited, and many attended, coming from near and far. No doubt many of the play's lines were silently mouthed throughout the audience that night! The after-party was held at a swanky nearby resto-bar – all champagne, strolling waiters with trays of hors d'oeuvres, a night of catching up and looking back. Saying goodbye to a unique and special stage experience. Throughout the evening, I kept thinking that the only mystery for me about this *Mousetrap* mystery was why it had taken me so long to become involved.

The first time someone asked me to direct a play took me by surprise. Actually, that's putting it lightly. Stunned or shocked probably better describe my reaction. Oh, I was instantly complimented and grateful that they felt I might know enough, had enough experience, and a solid enough grasp on the process of getting a show ready for an audience. And maybe the sensitivity and communication skills to support the actors as I shepherded them from first read-through to opening night. Because that's what being a director meant to me. I was amazed that someone felt comfortable that I might be able to do all those things, to *be* that person. I wasn't sure I was.

In all my years on stage, working in dozens and dozens of productions, I had never once thought about *directing* a show. As an actor, I was concerned with whatever role I was playing, any other characters I had to interact with, and the scenes I appeared in. The director had to see the big picture: they had to know about the arc of the story, how best to bring it to life using the stagecraft available, had to understand sometimes complex relationships between characters, and how to draw out the best performances from the players. There was the relentless hard work of rehearsing, intermittently having to detach, step back, and see what everything looked like from the audience's point of view. It seemed like a massive task, something formidable and mysterious. I thought about the many people who had directed me through the years – some I appreciated, some I wished for more from. There were the free spirits, the micro-managers, the kooks, the bullies. An infinite variety of styles and eccentricities …

David, who would leap up on stage every couple of pages to stand face-to-face right in front of an actor during rehearsal, following them through the blocking. He would maintain eye contact, ask pointed questions, deliver suggestions in the middle of the action – it could be very intense for the actor. There was no escape! Coming down off the stage, he'd be half-apologetic, explaining, "If I was more articulate, I'd be able to stay out of your way and tell you what I want from down here."

There was Marnie, who maintained that casting the right actors was 90% of her work, and if she did that right, they'd be able to basically direct themselves on stage. She'd sit through rehearsals, busying herself with knitting projects, calling out only once in a while to the players on stage. They may have expected a blocking change she wanted to see or an idea about a line-read, but were more likely to hear, "What do you think for the next stripe in this scarf – blue or green? The first time I worked with this director, I was taken aback never hearing a word or getting a bit of direction all the way through rehearsals. This was something new for me. I wondered if maybe she thought she had made a mistake casting me, that I was beyond help and she should just ignore me, until she could put it all behind her. Insecure, needy … just before curtain on opening night, I made a plea for any last-minute tidbit of help or advice. "Anything you'd like to tell me?" I asked. "Yeah. Just keep doing what you're doing. You crack me up!"

Working with Pascal was a whole other experience. He would either start a rehearsal with a prayer-huddle, or gather us in to bring our night's work to a close with some words of thanks. Amazingly, even cast members who joined in because it was expected, rolling their eyes at these practices to begin with, ended up being affected by the bonding and inspiration they offered (I know, because I was one!) Pascal built in mindfulness moments, where we were invited to practice compassion not only for ourselves as actors, but for our *characters*. It was about being present for our/their feelings and difficulties, sitting with any anxieties, sadness, anger, or whatever else was arising. A different way of working for sure.

Andrew brought years of experience as a well-respected, skilled performer along with him to the director's chair; he had a reputation as a brilliant comic actor. He proceeded to direct *every line of every character* exactly as he would play it. Intonation, body language, stage business, pauses, even facial gestures. There were some truly creative choices, but they weren't a good fit for every role or every actor. Most went along with whatever he shared, in the spirit of potentially absorbing some of his "genius." A few rebelled, provoking his "The theatre is not a DEMOCRACY!" rant. The show was solid and well-received, but prompted one audience member in-the-know to observe: "Good show. Certainly has Andrew's stink all over it." Backhanded compliment? Judgment? Who knows?!

James was a director who believed firmly in "animal work" as the key to constructing a character. Using this technique, the actor establishes the animal that feels closest to whatever role is being played, tries to understand its dynamic, then humanizes its physicality, its movement, and characteristics; this then informs the performance. I had been skeptical about this technique since being introduced to it at theatre school. During rehearsal, the director insisted that we stay in touch with our animal personas. I admit to having faked my choice, and was never sure if I should be fluttering like a sparrow, or leading with my forehead like a dolphin. If you couldn't uncover which was your animal, or perhaps settled on one the director felt was inappropriate, James came to the rescue. I recall vividly our dress rehearsal, when he shot up out of his seat like a lightning bolt in the middle of a scene. Nothing short of an epiphany: stopping the action on stage, he gestured dramatically towards one of the actors and shouted, "Patrick. Is. A. Mole!" (Phew, I guess we finally had the missing piece to that puzzle and could now sail confidently into our opening performance.)

If I decided to accept the director's job, I knew I'd want to be like ALL of those directors I had worked with! To be the *best* parts of all of them. Because regardless of their individual ways of working, their quirks, and idiosyncrasies, they each managed to guide a company from table-read through to audience-ready show. I suppose I might have looked at directing as a step in my evolution as a theatre artist (oh man, that sounds so affected …) Like a hockey player becoming the team coach or a teacher coming up through the ranks to take over as school principal. A giant undertaking. I signed on and hoped I was up to the challenge.

I didn't get to start from scratch with my first production; it was a three-hander and I "inherited" the cast. I think they were friends of the producer and had been promised roles. Were they the actors I would have cast in those roles? Probably not. (Would I ever again agree to direct a show I hadn't cast? Probably not.) But I had worked on stage long enough to have an intimate understanding of the acting process – to be able to grasp the action and character arcs in a personalized way - and felt confident that I could communicate and support these performers in telling the story. I knew that the big-picture view was an important aspect of directing and I had a clear vision for the show as a whole. I did my script analysis, broke the play down into scenes, and worked out the blocking before we ever met for rehearsal. It was a fringe show: one act, with a minimalist set, just a couple of pieces of furniture and a few props. Working through the scenes was exciting: we figured out a lot during our two weeks together, and although these were not ideally who I would have had playing the roles, there were no ego clashes or difficult personalities. I started to feel like I might – just *might* – be on the road to figuring it out.

Then it was time for our tech rehearsal. Fringe productions are allotted one technical run-through with the lighting and sound staff at whatever theatre a show has been assigned. One run-through where everything is set. Of course I had thought about the various effects I envisioned. But sitting alone in the darkened theatre that day, script in hand, trying to call out my wishes and needs to unseen lighting and sound experts up in the control booth was another matter. It was daunting. I had neither the language nor the detail required to be helpful or answer their questions.

"House to half to lights up ... how many seconds?"
"Do you want to bring up your show music as we fade the house?"
"So ... a cooler hue while the letter is being read?"
"Shutters, maybe? Are you thinking we need to shape

the light on your actor here?"

I stumbled through, and thanks only to the patience and know-how of the resident crew, we ended up with a show that was professionally lit and sounded great. A huge lesson and a reminder that it wasn't all about the actors! For a director, telling the story involves not only bringing out the best in the onstage talent, but knowing how to work with design, lighting, sound, and costuming people. I determined that if I ever took on another directing assignment, I had to be better prepared for that collaboration.

I wasn't sure anyone would take a chance on me again as a director, or sure if I had the guts to be at the helm of another show ... but weeks later, a new opportunity presented itself. I said yes! It was a bigger deal, directing Edward Albee's A *Delicate Balance* for a community theatre group. This time I did get to cast my own actors, which was kind of surreal. Listening to people read, taking notes, being in the position of deciding who was right for a role, what actors were a good match to play opposite each other. I had always been on the other side of the casting table, working to impress, hoping to snag a part. (Eye-opening insights seeing everything from this turn-about perspective: intel that I knew would impact the way I auditioned going forward!) And this time I was aware of what I *didn't* know about the technical and design elements, and worked with an experienced stage manager who helped me navigate those aspects. I knew I needed to communicate to the tech people the essence of the production, as well as the artistic goals I wanted to achieve, so they could put their expertise and creative insights to work to support the storytelling. Three months of rehearsals with highs, lows, and lots of learning for me personally. The experience was satisfying enough that I took on another show, and another after that, and started to find my own way as a director. To figure out what was important to me and how I liked to work with the actors. Because that was where I felt most comfortable; that was always my favourite part of the equation.

The first read-through, or table read, as it's sometimes called, is just so everyone can become familiar with the story we're going to tell. At this point, I ask for "no acting." Sometimes actors arrive, ready to impress by delivering fully-realized characterizations. Vocal choices, nuances of tone, and rapport with other characters all set. They've done their homework and are eager to show they're the right person for the role. Gotta give them credit for reading the entire script beforehand and giving some thought to what their part entails. The trouble with prematurely presenting a full-blown performance like this is that it closes off the actor to some of the gifts of rehearsing - understanding motivation and relationship, and organically growing a believable character. If actors come in with too many preconceived ideas, which they may be quite attached to (they've done a lot of work on their own to get there!) – it can be hard to strip away these notions if they don't truly serve the play. My "no acting" ask doesn't always take, but it's how I like to start the work.

As a director, I feel it's up to me to set the emotional tone of rehearsals. I want to create a safe, collaborative space where actors are willing to try things, to experiment, even to let themselves look foolish at times. Actors who feel they always have to be in control and have everything figured out don't give themselves a chance to grow and change through the three weeks or three months or however long the rehearsal period is. I definitely want them to feel like *contributors*. A well-known adage maintains that at the first rehearsal the director knows more about the characters than the players do ... but by the last rehearsal, they know more about their characters than the director does. It makes sense: they're the ones doing the intense study, getting inside the head and heart of their characters. Having said that, I also need my actors to trust me and be open to my contribution. If I ask them to try something ... I want them to *try it!* Hearing "My character wouldn't do that," or "That's the way my character would say that line" is not helpful. Humour me! Try it! We'll see if it's awkward or doesn't work or isn't an improvement. And we can laugh about it and toss it out. But what if it *does* work, and we discover something new or cool or surprising together? This is the atmosphere I want to create for us all to work in.

I always did my advance blocking to ensure flow, to emphasize aspects of plot and relationship, and to create an effective stage picture. I stayed connected with my actors as they rehearsed to bring the story to life. Still, there would be places where things just didn't seem to come together, where something in a scene was missing or "wrong" or needed fixing. It's the director's concern, but the director doesn't always have the solution. I had worked with directors who simply shifted the responsibility by saying, "It's an actor's problem. Solve it!" Then they would criticize and show their dissatisfaction and disappointment if the actors weren't able to figure it all out. Actors would feel inadequate, which of course was counterproductive. And unfair. Something G.B. Shaw said in his book, *The Art of Rehearsal*, stuck in my mind: he advised directors not to mention things that weren't working to actors "in a heartbroken and desperate way, as if the world were crumbling in ruins." I knew what it felt like when directors did that and vowed never to do that to my actors. If I didn't know how to make something better, I said nothing. At the same time (with great difficulty), I tried to take the pressure off myself as the person in charge to know everything, to be able to fix everything. We just kept working until together we found the right thing to do. And sometimes we never did. That's just how it went.

Did I like directing? It was an education for sure! And certainly rewarding. Would I ever choose it over acting in a production? A hard "No." My least favourite thing was feeling redundant ... superfluous ... not needed once a show was up and running. The director's job is over: you've guided your players, your team, your flock – they can fly on their own! They move on without you. The director is no longer part of that tight-knit show family once opening night happens. And I missed that a lot.

So of course, I was once again consumed with tracking down a new on-stage adventure! I was ready. Where would I get to play again, to take on another role, to spend some hours doing work I loved? And when? No agent, no union card, no big master plan. Just keeping my ear to the ground, putting myself out there, creating the endless self-tapes that had become the norm for auditioning by 2023 ... The forever-hustle, or as I call it, "Welcome to my life." Following that long ago wished-for dream of moments in that little pool of light ...

ACKNOWLEDGMENTS

I'm grateful for the privilege of working with all the actors, directors, and teachers who've delighted, puzzled, and inspired me over the years. Without them there would be no story to tell. Some names have been changed for the sake of privacy (although people who were around during those times will no doubt recognize the players!)

How fortunate am I to have had the support and assistance of my sister, Pamela and my daughter, Meagan - both writers as well - as I cobbled together these stories! Their intelligence and sense of humour have been pretty terrific. And my daughter's generosity in formatting my manuscript was a vital gift to low-tech me.

Finally, thank you, dear reader, for picking up my book and stepping in for a bit to my life as a working actor!

www.ingramcontent.com/pod-product-compliance
Lightning Source LLC
Chambersburg PA
CBHW051601010526
44118CB00023B/2773